The Kindness Workbook

An Interactive Guide for Creating Compassion in Yourself and the World

Robin Raven

ADAMS MEDIA

NEW YORK LONDON TORONTO SYDNEY NEW DELHI

adamsmedia

Adams Media
An Imprint of Simon & Schuster, Inc.
100 Technology Center Drive
Stoughton, Massachusetts 02072

First Adams Media trade paperback edition December 2021

ADAMS MEDIA and colophon are trademarks of Simon & Schuster.

For information about special discounts for bulk purchases, please contact Simon & Schuster Special Sales at 1-866-506-1949 or business@simonandschuster.com.

The Simon & Schuster Speakers Bureau can bring authors to your live event. For more information or to book an event contact the Simon & Schuster Speakers Bureau at 1-866-248-3049 or visit our website at www.simonspeakers.com.

Interior design by Alaya Howard

Interior images © 123RF/Aquamarine1paint, tisti
Hand lettering by Priscilla Yuen

Manufactured in the United States of America

1 2021

ISBN 978-1-5072-1728-3

*This book is dedicated to my dear friend
and mentor, Jerry Houser.*

*Jerry, thanks for teaching me so much
about the human capacity for kindness
and inspiring me to appreciate
all the wonder in this world.*

CONTENTS

PART TWO 85

Introduction

Kindness can change the world and empower you to live a more joyful and fulfilling life. And while random acts of kindness are a wonderful way to spread good in the world, fostering actual social connection is even more powerful. The Kindness Workbook *will help you do just that by showing you the steps you can take to be kinder to yourself and spread that kindness to others as well.*

Practicing kindness for just a few minutes every day helps you think more positively and lovingly toward yourself and others. *The Kindness Workbook* will walk you through ninety-five reflective exercises, fun activities, mindful meditations, and more, helping you incorporate kindness into your life on many levels. Some of the activities will focus on your internal journey to kindness, and others will focus on going out and putting that kindness into action. Feel free to flip through these pages and choose the type of kindness activity that matches your mood and motivation level for the day. Each entry also features a "Keep It Going!" section, where you'll see how you can take the lessons you've learned on kindness and actively integrate them into your daily life.

Whichever type of activity you choose, you'll find that by practicing kindness your life can change in positive ways. You'll feel calmer, less stressed, more compassionate, and more tolerant. Best of all, your kindness will spread to others who may take up a kindness practice of their own, which can start the cycle of kindness all over again, and help kick-start a positive ripple effect extending out into the world.

This book will help you discover more about your innate kindness and how to share it with yourself and others effectively. Just like muscles that strengthen when they are used, your capacity for compassion can grow stronger the more you exercise it—and *The Kindness Workbook* will be there with you to help each step of the way.

How to Use This Book

Before you start your journey with kindness, here are a few things to consider:

- Approach each exercise with an open mind and heart. That doesn't mean that every action will resonate with you. However, try to participate in each activity and see how it feels. You just might nurture some new positive habits and curate some new methods for spreading kindness.
- Although the exercises build on each other, there is no specific order that you have to follow. Feel free to skip around in the workbook and do activities that feel right to you.
- Grab a notebook and keep a daily journal as you strive to manifest more kindness in your life. It's fun to look back over time and see a great deal of progress.
- Color-coding different types of notes may help you keep things organized, so you might want to grab a pack of pens with a rainbow of colors. Add your thoughts, feelings, and creativity in any way you want to make this all your own.

- This may be a "work" book, but it shouldn't feel like work! Have fun with the exercises and look for the ways that you connect to the activities. Want to tweak them slightly? Go for it. They're here to serve you.

Acknowledging these key points should help you have an experience that's enjoyable and successful. A cool thing about kindness is that it's infinitely renewable. There are no limits to the services a life can hold. The more empathy you spread, the more you may inspire others to do kind things too. On that merry note, let's get started!

PART ONE

Be Kinder to Yourself

In this first part, you'll find some practical steps to be kinder and gentler with yourself. That, in turn, should help you live a fuller life that's overflowing with the rewards that kindness brings. When you treat yourself like the VIP you are, you can more easily be kind to those around you.

Silence Your Inner Critic

For your loving-kindness to grow and flourish, start by being gentle with yourself. Think about all the ways you've made others' lives better, easier, and more fun through your past acts of kindness. Revel in the joy that gave you. Now think of how you could make your own life better, easier, and more fun. You are just as important, and you deserve it too.

One way that you can best nurture yourself with kindness is to speak gently to yourself. The inner critic in everybody tends to leap to unfair, absolute conclusions. Turn that around by trying to talk to yourself with compassion, the same way you would talk to a dear friend who's in pain.

Here's an example. Consider someone who makes an impulsive purchase and then tells themself, "You screwed up again! You're terrible with money." Compare that to someone who instead says, "Okay, this is one mistake. Let's move forward with a smart choice that can help balance things out." The second solution helps you efficiently move on from a mistake and channel your energy into positive solutions.

Now consider this: How can you better show yourself loving-kindness when you most need it? Start by replacing negative things you often tell yourself with compassionate and constructive things instead. Then, in the following space, write what you would usually say to yourself and jot down kinder alternatives.

The harsh thing you told yourself:

What you can say instead:

The harsh thing you told yourself:

What you can say instead:

The harsh thing you told yourself:

What you can say instead:

Try this for one week and delight in how much more manageable and pleasurable life can get when you lavish kindness on yourself. Do this until being gentler to yourself feels comfortable. Then, if you forget what you want to say, just return to these pages and read your solutions.

You have the power to create the future you want with one kind word and thought at a time.

Keep It Going! These steps can be the start of a more peaceful, loving way of empowering yourself to live your best life. But first, make a real commitment to talk to yourself gently every day.

Make Sensory Connections

Your senses help you experience and perceive the world around you. For thousands of years, we have known about the five basic senses: hearing, smell, taste, touch, and sight. However, neuroscientists now generally agree that humans have several other senses, such as the sense of heat and balance perception.

Nurturing your body, mind, and spirit through the senses is one way of showing basic, primal kindness to yourself. So, let's celebrate the wonder of the human body's senses and the power they have to inspire you to be happier, calmer, and kinder.

Look at the following list of senses. Consider all the feelings they inspire. Acknowledge each sense and indulge it. Then, choose a related activity that makes you feel good. For smell, you might walk in a botanical garden where you can take in whiffs of your favorite floral fragrances, or savor a bubble bath with scented bath salts.

This exercise will focus on seven senses, but you can add any you want. Feel free to substitute any of the senses listed with another one.

- Taste
- Smell
- Touch
- Sight
- Hearing
- Balance Perception
- Heat

Keep It Going! We know our senses work collaboratively within the mind and body. Try indulging multiple senses at once and see how you feel.

Nurture Self-Love Through Esteemed Acts

You are extraordinary! You deserve your affection, and you don't need to wait a moment for someone else to lavish love on you. But, before you can fully accept others' love, you need to love yourself fully and effectively. That is the root of showing kindness to yourself and the world.

So, how can you feel a strong, joy-inducing sense of love for yourself? What you choose to do each day will directly impact how you feel about yourself, and acting in a way that honors your values will nourish your soul.

Think about loving things you can do for yourself and others. Then go out and do them one thing at a time. As you start this endeavor, draw the simple shape of a stone on a piece of paper. Within it, write the first thing you do to nurture yourself. Next, draw another stone and add the next item. Do this until you have an entire wall on the paper, with each stone representing one building block for fully loving yourself. Before you know it, you will have a wall of loving acts. Look at how you have the power to create love and kindness in the world!

Keep It Going! You may want to make a photocopy of your drawing and hang it up in a place where you can see and reflect on it each morning. Recommit to doing kind acts every day!

Guided Meditation: Accept and Cultivate Kindnesses

Close your eyes for a moment and imagine what a perfect world looks like to you. How does kindness manifest itself in that ideal world? What matters the most to you there? With meditation, you have the power to connect your mind, body, and spirit with the ideals that are closest to your heart. So, with this meditation, you'll focus on cultivating loving-kindness and extending it to yourself and others.

Let's get started.

1. Choose a corner of your home to be a calming haven. Enhance it with pillows, scented candles, and soothing works of art to set the scene for a place of peace. Now sit down and allow your body to simply be. Accept any feelings that wash over you.
2. Take a deep breath. Inhale and exhale slowly. Try to be in the moment and feel the sensations of each breath as it enters your body. How does that make every part of your body feel? Try to connect with your body and increase your awareness from head to toe.
3. Continue to inhale and exhale slowly and deeply. Now try to think of a person who recently made you happy with their kindness. As this awareness inspires you, don't judge any thought or feeling that comes up. Trust your heart and what it feels. Imagine the person, and consider how this awareness makes you feel inside. Remind yourself that you deserve the kindness they showed you.

4. Send love to whom you envision. Now imagine they are sending it back to you. Imagine yourself receiving strong waves of loving-kindness.
5. Inhale and exhale through your mouth while trying to visualize the continuation of that loving-kindness. What does it look like? Try to envision yourself sending love to people, places, and even situations.
6. Repeat steps 2–5 over and over again. Stay in the sensations of loving-kindness. Set a timer if you have limited time, but make sure to give yourself at least ten minutes for this meditation—you deserve your full attention. Trust yourself to make any adjustments to help you feel more comfortable and more empowered with each practice.

Keep It Going! Try to cultivate a daily meditation practice on kindness for a few weeks. If you are feeling inspired by it, consider expanding the practice even longer.

Develop Morning Affirmations

Affirmations are simple statements that spark positive feelings within you. They can also amplify your motivations. Affirmations that encourage acts of kindness are constructive, because they create a cycle of good that spreads joy.

Start creating affirmations as a regular part of your routine. After all, it's easier for things to go right when you prepare to embrace all the wonder a day can hold. So, set yourself up for success. Read the following examples of affirmations and highlight or underline the ones that resonate with you. You may not feel like you fully embody each declaration, but they can encourage you to accept and embrace actions to make each statement a reality.

I have an open heart that's ready to receive infinite kindness.

I love myself fully and completely.

I am a beautiful human being.

I am worthy of love and kindness.

I am a better person today than I was yesterday.

I have an abundance of compassion in my heart.

Now it's your turn to create your original morning affirmations. Think of your ideal goals for each day and what you need to be your kindest self. Then write them in the following space.

As you repeat these affirmations each morning, you may find yourself wanting to tweak them and adjust the things you say. That's a good thing. It means they are actively becoming a part of your daily inner dialogue. Trust yourself, and adapt them as often as you want.

Keep It Going! Continue creating new affirmations as you determine what most inspires kindness within you.

Reimagine Your Ticket to Mean Cinema

Have you ever criticized yourself over some unkind thoughts that passed through your mind? That's natural, but it's a waste of energy. Instead, try to see your ideas the way you would a movie. Heroes and villains interact. There are heroic actions and dastardly misdeeds. Whatever wins out is the result of a screenwriter's choice.

In large part, you are the screenwriter of the script of your own life. The thoughts you have aren't good or bad. The actions you take because of those thoughts most certainly can be, though. Take responsibility for the consequences of your choices and actions. You should, however, forgive yourself for negative, judgmental, and mean thoughts.

It's even okay to visualize a mean scenario playing out in your imagination. You don't want to dwell there too long, but unkind thoughts don't necessarily translate into cold actions. A thought can never really be good or bad until you give it power.

Roughly draw a few movie tickets in the following space. On each one, write any mean or negative thought you might have. As you jot the thought down, imagine it leaving your mind. Then use dark-colored crayons to color over the thought to show just how fleeting and meaningless a stray thought is. After all, the mean thought can quickly be replaced by something lovely. Next, grab a marker and write a kind or loving thought on the ticket instead.

Keep It Going! Try not to judge any thoughts that come through your mind. Remind yourself of this exercise and how quickly your perspective can change.

Fill Your Treasure Chest

What is most important to you? If you could have anything your loving heart desires, what would it be? Would it be money? True love? The support and understanding of your partner? The highest award within your profession? More followers on social media? One memorable day with those you love without drama or worries? A specific gift for your birthday?

The specifics of what you most want in this world will be unique to you, and nearly anything goes! These can be tangible and intangible things. There are no right or wrong answers here. Also, know this: You have more power than you think to fulfill your wishes and give your heart what it wants. Later, you can consider your heart's desires and decide what you realistically want to pursue in the real world.

This is a time for dreaming and wishing. Trust your instincts and desires. Envision a treasure chest in the future that you have filled as you made your dreams come true. What would it hold? Think of mementos of awesome experiences or physical treasures you want to acquire. As you imagine what you most want, write it down here.

_____

_____

_____

_____

_____

_____

_____

_____

_____

_____

_____

When you are personally fulfilled, you are in the best position to share joy and kindness with others. If you feel happy and satisfied, it's much easier to wish the best for others. Taking care of yourself and making your dreams come true are the cornerstones of kindness that you show yourself. That, in turn, inspires kindness to others. So, take pride in making your dreams come true. You deserve your success!

Keep It Going! As you continue through this workbook, you may realize some things you left out of your treasure chest. Feel free to come back and add more.

Check In with Yourself

Take the time to connect with yourself on a deep level each day. That's an act of loving consciousness to help you appreciate yourself and others more. It will also enable you to connect more deeply with your inner capacity for kindness.

Take a deep breath, then express how you feel right here in this moment. Jot down the first and most prominent thoughts you have here.

_____

_____

_____

_____

Take another deep breath. Hold it in for a few seconds, then exhale. Now become aware of what is around you. What are you most aware of right now? How does this awareness make you feel?

_____

_____

_____

After you express what you feel in this moment, delve deeper to uncover what makes you think the way you do right now. For example, if you feel frustrated by the color red, what memories does that color bring up? What were you doing in the most potent memory that surfaces? What did the room you were in smell like? What was the weather like? Try to keep going deeper with the thoughts and

feelings that come up. Before you can be fully present, you first need to acknowledge and explore the thoughts and feelings that are active for you beyond this moment. Dealing with all of these things will significantly impact your capacity for kindness at any given moment. We're at our most kind and loving when we are fully present in the moment. So, write down what you are aware of right now.

_____

_____

_____

_____

Now check in one more time. Do you feel fully in the present now? If not, further explore what is on your mind and what you need to be focused on the present moment. What do you need to truly and fully be right here, right now, with no distractions?

_____

_____

_____

_____

Knowing your thoughts and feelings can help you realize which inner need you must fulfill, so you can remove yourself from any frustrating situation before acting in a way you may regret.

Keep It Going! Whenever you are about to lose your temper with someone or otherwise unleash unkindness, take a few moments to check in with yourself. See what's going on.

Keep Your Batteries Charged

When you feel good inside, it's easier to live your best life and be your best self. On the other hand, it can be challenging to spread kindness to others when you're burned out. That's all the more reason to take fantastic care of yourself. Prevent burnout when it comes to service by doing many nice things for yourself to refresh and replenish.

Self-care can take the form of nearly anything. Here are some popular ideas for self-care you may enjoy. Highlight or circle ones that are likely to make you feel refreshed and recharged.

 Relax in a bubble bath.

Take a stroll in the park.

Go for a drive with the windows down.

 Listen to your favorite album from childhood.

Have a snack that's both tasty and healthy.

Set aside an hour just to read something fun.

 Turn on a fast-paced song and shake your body to the rhythm.

Sign up to learn something you always wanted to try.

Cancel flexible plans to take a nap.

 Sing the first song that comes to your mind.

Now, try to think of other things that would give you a significant boost. What would make you feel like a new person or at least a renewed one? In the following space, write down all the things you enjoy doing that leave you feeling invigorated and energized. Try not to second-guess or judge the things that make you feel this way. Instead, celebrate them. These are kind things you can do for yourself, and that can ricochet to kindness for others.

Keep It Going! Bookmark this page and reflect on it for the next several days, weeks, and even months. Every time you think of a new re-energizing activity, come back and write about it here.

Rewrite a Bad Day

Some bad days are easier to shake off than others. Any hurt or sadness is valid, and you shouldn't try to minimize any melancholy feeling. Acknowledge bad feelings when they come along. While you shouldn't deny the truth about a day that's less than stellar, you don't have to give in to the negativity of a bad day. You deserve to put it behind you, and have a good day tomorrow!

Use the following space to write about the last time you had a miserable day.

If you have a bad day, try to consider what could have made it better. In some situations, evaluating what went wrong can help you make different choices for happier outcomes next time! Of course, you often can't control what causes a bad day, but you can choose how you react to it. What choices could you have made differently throughout the last bad day you experienced?

What did you learn from that bad day? What are the ways that you want to take personal responsibility for having a good day? What are things beyond your control?

What can you do to help avoid a downward spiral the next time you have a bad day?

Keep It Going! Try to continue to evaluate the bad days to see how you can help make them better! Comforting yourself and learning from your mistakes shows great compassion for yourself.

Pretend You'll Live Forever

Would you live forever if you could? Just think of all the things that could be possible if you were never going to leave the world. Maybe having an eternity to fulfill your dreams would make it easier to relax more often. On the other hand, perhaps the concept of endless time would inspire you to fill it with meaningful moments. Consider all the ways your life would change if you weren't limited to a typical human lifetime.

Although you may not be able to actually live forever, researchers from the University of California, Los Angeles (UCLA) Bedari Kindness Institute revealed that kindness can increase longevity. Some studies even show that people who volunteer live longer than those who don't. Talk about a good deal! When you give, you get so much in return.

Imagine you could suddenly live forever. What would you change right away? Should you go ahead and make that change now, even though you cannot predict the future?

If you were living forever, what are three things you think you would want to continue doing every day into infinity? What are three kindnesses you see yourself sustaining indefinitely? These are things you want to integrate into your life now. Reflect on how you might find a way to start doing them daily.

_____

_____

_____

_____

_____

Imagining that you know you'll live forever, write about what you would do in the following space.

_____

_____

_____

_____

_____

_____

_____

Keep It Going! Asking yourself about imaginary situations can help you see kindness in new and exciting ways. That can also help bring new ways of showing compassion into clear focus.

Nurture Daily Habits to Optimize Kindness

Happy habits that lead to an abundance of kindness in your life don't form in a bubble. They are a part of each day's complex puzzle that can help you create the life you want! First, you need to choose and commit to them. Beyond that, positive habits become an active, living part of your life when you decide to create and nurture them.

Start by going through your day as an observer. Do this on a day when you plan to stick to your routine. Then, throughout the day, make notes about what is missing from your day. Also, jot down observations about what you could do to make life easier on yourself or those closest to you. What problems come up? Do those problems happen often? What could you start doing every day to prevent them from happening again? Is there a habit you might add to your day that would help others you encounter? Be as specific as possible.

Think about the new habits that you could start to help your day go better. Consider the habits that would be meaningful to you. Contemplate the actions you'd be comfortable taking to make life better for you and others. Then write down the new habits you want to form in the space that follows.

Now choose one habit that you want to implement into your day right away. After a week of getting used to that habit, add the next one. Come back until you have integrated all these chosen habits into your life. Your new habits need to be an active, dynamic part of your life each day. While it can be a challenge to make lasting changes in your life, you can do it! It gets easier and easier as you adjust to the new habits too!

_____

_____

_____

_____

_____

_____

_____

_____

_____

_____

_____

_____

Keep It Going! After you form these new habits, you may want to add others. Keep assessing and adjusting your habits to serve you and others best!

Draw and Dream: Remember Your First Kindnesses

Your experiences in early childhood can have a profound impact on the rest of your life. Your foundational experiences likely shaped your views on kindness. Drive along memory lane to think about those first brushes with compassion and understanding.

Savoring good memories can help propel you forward. Consider all the ways you were nurtured as a young child. Who was there for you? What did you understand about treating others with gentleness? Were you willing to share? Was it fun to give presents to loved ones? Try to think of times when you felt joyful because of nice things that your parents or siblings did for you. Go back to the thrilling moments when people outside your family showed that they loved you too.

What was your first awareness of kindness? Think of your first memory of someone doing something extraordinarily kind for you. How old were you? What did it feel like? Think about the memory and draw it in the following space. As you draw, reflect on the wonder of those moments and how good it felt to be on the receiving end of kindness.

This gentle focus on wonderful moments may inspire you to reach out and thank the person responsible, or maybe you want to repeat this experience for someone else. Follow your inspiration after you draw, and dwell on, this lovely memory.

Keep It Going! Make a habit of reflecting on memories of good deeds. It can help fuel your momentum to spread love and kindness.

Take a Step in the Right Direction

Each decision that you make in life can have an impact on your future in some way. Even when some choices seem small, move forward with the most compassionate options whenever possible. A series of small steps can ultimately lead you to where you want to be.

In keeping with the symbolic steps of this activity, draw a simple staircase in the space that follows. It doesn't need to be detailed. You just want to give yourself space to write on each step.

Now think of something you want to do for someone you love. It could be something as simple as buying a lovely gift or planning a party; it could be more complex, like helping your loved one achieve a goal or supporting them in recovering from an illness. Identify the purpose and write it at the top of the staircase you've drawn.

Now, starting at the bottom step, write down one thing you can do that will bring you closer to completing the act of kindness you chose. The first step doesn't have to be something grand. It can be as simple as reaching out to your friend to ask them what kind of support you can offer them today.

Then, on the next step, write the next action you can take to get closer to the goal. Working your way up the staircase, keep writing down which actions you need to take one step at a time. If you need more steps, add them. When you finish filling in the drawing, you should have identified what you need to do to achieve your goal, and you'll have clearly stated steps to get to where you want to go.

As you do this exercise, visualize yourself completing the goal, and reflect on how good it will feel to achieve it.

Keep It Going! Examine the possibilities before you make any decision. Doing so can often prevent mistakes and stop you from doing unkind things.

Choose to Lose

When you are kind to yourself, you are going to lose some things, but that's good news! Sometimes we work really hard to get something that seems special, only to realize that it doesn't give us an ounce of joy. It's important to be able to assess what does and doesn't make your life better. If something in your life is more trouble than it's worth, that's a sign that you need to let it go. Simply release it for your well-being.

Take a moment to consider all the things in your life that you would be better off without. What might be positive for someone else may be negative for you. Look at the following list and consider whether you want to let any of these things go from your own life. In the blank space after the list, write other things you want to let go of.

- **Self-doubt:** A little can be a good thing, but too much can sabotage your confidence.
- **Complaining about the small stuff:** Everyone should be able to vent and get out their feelings, but excessively sweating the small stuff doesn't serve any purpose.
- **Spending time with people who don't appreciate you:** Letting go of people who don't care frees up space in your life for those who will cherish you.
- **Fixating on the past:** When you struggle to let things go, therapy can work wonders to help you process and release past traumas.
- **Unrealistic expectations:** Great expectations are reasonable—just not ones that are too big!
- **Procrastination:** Sometimes you need to put off a task, but chronic procrastination can put a huge wedge between you and your goals.

_____

_____

_____

_____

_____

_____

_____

_____

_____

_____

_____

_____

_____

_____

_____

_____

_____

Keep It Going! As you go through life, try to be honest with
yourself when something that seems like a good thing isn't making
you happy. If it's no longer serving you, let it go.

Own Your Dreams and Desires

Your wildest dreams don't have to be outrageous, and you don't have to have your head in the clouds to have a lot of dreams. Some people feel that they have a calling from the time they are small children, while others choose careers based on practical choices rather than a passion. Your dreams may have little to do with your career and everything to do with how you want to live or what you want to enjoy in your spare time.

Start by thinking about which dreams and desires are at the forefront of your mind. What are some of your unfulfilled needs? Could others in your life help you meet those needs? What is your own innermost need when it comes to your professional life? How might kindness transform your career or make you happier?

Brainstorm and write down some unfulfilled dreams and desires that are important to you. After writing down five important goals, write one way that acts of kindness can connect you to what you most want. Does it involve asking for help or simply being kind to yourself? Be candid about what needs to happen. Next, think about how you might feel when you're able to have your needs met and live with these things in your life. This will help you stay motivated to bridge your wishes to what it will take to fulfill them.

When you are kind to yourself and willing to ask for help from others, you'll find that your life is better and that your relationships are likely strengthened. You deserve to thrive and have your needs met. Show up for yourself and make it happen!

Keep It Going! After you make these dreams come true, repeat this practice with new wishes that will pop up over time.

Manifest Your Values

Being clear on your values and staying true to them can inspire self-respect and the manifestation of love and kindness. Your values should reflect the way you want to live your life, who you are, and how you aspire to be. While like-minded people may share similar ethics, everyone needs to decide for themselves what they want to prioritize in life.

Certain traits may help you forge kindness or otherwise inspire you to live in an ethically sound way. Consider this list of values and think about how important each one is to you. Put a check mark by the values that matter most to you.

- Acceptance
- Altruism
- Balance
- Bravery
- Compassion
- Confidence
- Dedication
- Discipline
- Empathy
- Enjoyment
- Fortitude
- Friendship
- Generosity
- Gratitude
- Happiness
- Hope
- Independence
- Intelligence
- Joy
- Kindness
- Love
- Loyalty
- Moderation
- Neatness
- Open-Mindedness
- Organization
- Patience
- Power
- Quality
- Reliability
- Respect
- Sacrifice
- Self-Control
- Talent
- Transparency
- Understanding
- Unity
- Victory
- Vision
- Winning
- Wisdom

Think about how each of the values you selected can contribute to creating kindness in the world. Now think about whether any might simultaneously block acts of kindness. Are any neutral? How might specific values interact and strengthen each other?

Now consider what your all-time top values are. Write them in the space that follows. Some of these values may be in the previous list, or they may be something else entirely.

Keep It Going! Whenever you meet someone living their life in a way you admire, ask them about their values. You may be inspired to revise your priorities from time to time!

Create Constellations of Kindness

Which feelings do the following kindness-related words inspire in you?

- Affection
- Warmth
- Generosity
- Volunteer

- Care
- Love
- Protection
- Humane

- Tolerance
- Tenderness
- Compassion
- Good

Do these words conjure any visual images in your mind? Try to focus only on one word at a time and really zero in on the significance of that word. Think about the memories the word conjures in your mind and any way it resonates with what's going on with you today. Also think about what you want the word to mean for you in the future.

Imagine which visual symbols you would use for each word. Then, in the space provided, draw a connect-the-stars constellation to symbolize four of the words that resonate most strongly with you. For example, for the word *love*, you may choose to draw a constellation of a heart or something else that's personally meaningful to you.

Visualization can inspire a new way to connect with a thought or idea. Consider other words that you associate with kindness and try to connect them with a visual symbol too. How do you embody these words? What ways do you want them to be a part of your life? Reflecting during your visualizations can help you connect more fully to the concepts and the feelings they inspire.

Keep It Going! If you keep a journal or practice meditation, you may add visualization and drawing what you envision as part of your relaxation process.

Vent Your Way to Good Feelings

If you've ever been told to "make the best of it" or "look on the bright side," you have probably suffered with the irritation that toxic positivity can cause. Yes, it is a wonderful thing to nurture a positive outlook. However, denying your negative feelings may cause far more problems than feeling sad ever could. Before you are ready to make the best of any situation, it's good to get real about how you fully feel about the one you're currently in.

In the spirit of honoring the many parts of yourself and the numerous complex feelings that come naturally to every human being, here's permission to complain. Perhaps you've been conditioned to not complain or express your gripes. You're formally invited to forget that nonsense and level with yourself about every feeling you currently have. (Here's a secret: That'll actually help you get rid of them a lot faster!)

You probably hold space in your life for your friends to vent. Now it's time to hold space in your life to allow yourself that same luxury. Here's your chance to get out any negative thought or feeling you may have been struggling to ignore. Was someone mean to you? What did you really want to say to them? Express it here. Get it all out. It's okay. What do you hate about yourself? What regrets do you have? What are you insecure about? Yep, that belongs here too.

_____

_____

_____

_____

_____

_____

_____

_____

_____

_____

_____

_____

_____

_____

_____

_____

_____

Whew, do you feel better? When you move through the negative feelings, you can more fully enjoy the positive feelings that are sure to follow. If you are in therapy, share the things you've written here with your therapist. It's a great way to get real with yourself. Now that you have released these feelings, you are free to color over them with a black crayon or keep them here as a reminder of how getting out your feelings can be helpful.

Keep It Going! Try to start a journal in which you are completely honest. Write in it whenever you feel any strong emotions.

Choose Your Monthly Theme Word

Some people choose one word on January 1 to symbolize the entire year ahead of them. That's a pretty big commitment. However, the practice is appealing. It allows you to have one simple focus for a specific amount of time. Let's try that on a smaller scale.

For the next month, what do you want to accomplish? What do you want to attract in your life? What do you want to happen in your relationships? Are there any purchases you want to make? What is the best way you can be kind to yourself over the next month?

When you have answered these questions for yourself, consider what your biggest priority is for the next thirty or thirty-one days. This priority should be something tangible that you can achieve, not something like winning the lottery. It should be something you have at least a significant amount of control over. It also needs to be a way of lavishing kindness on yourself.

Now, what one word would best serve as a symbol of that priority? For example, if you want to learn how to ride a bike but are afraid of falling off the bike, you may choose the word *courage* as your word of the month. You will need courage to follow through with a goal like that.

In the space that follows, write the word you chose in bubble letters, then color them in. You may also write two or three ways that you can carry out actions that are aligned with your word of the month each day.

Keep It Going! Continue to choose a new word each month! It can be a fun way to motivate yourself to succeed with achievable, short-term goals.

Create Your Own Kindness Book Club

"Being good isn't good enough." An anonymous person started spreading that quote around the Internet, and it's caused some confusion. What does it mean exactly? It's open for interpretation, but many people think that it simply means that you need to "walk the walk" and "talk the talk." In doing so, you'll realize so much of your potential for kindness!

One way to be a better person is to understand the complex dynamics of the current world we live in. It's important to be sensitive to others' feelings, and that can be hard to do if we don't understand them. In that spirit, form your own kindness book club. Gather books that you need to read to better comprehend things that are beyond your current understanding. Include anti-racism books, books about other cultures, inspirational books, and other books to help you be a more informed human who can better support and engage with others.

Next, make a list of the books in the space that follows, take a picture of it, and share it on social media and ask your friends to join you. That's a great way to spread awareness of authors and activists who are doing the work of making the world a better place. Amplifying the voices of authors is a great kindness, and it's a win-win situation, because your social media friends and followers will benefit from participating too. You can help increase tolerance and kindness with each post about your book club!

Keep It Going! Continue your book club all year long. Keep learning about new authors and books that may help increase your understanding of all those who share the world with you.

Notice Your Focus

What do you notice the most about life as you go about your day? If you watch the news or true-crime documentaries, you may see that there are enough horrors in the world to fill an eternal loop of scary movies. On the flip side of that, people are performing wonderful, selfless acts of compassion every moment of the day. Between the extremes, think beyond the gray to notice every other color of the rainbow. There is a huge spectrum of lovely things people do for one another.

For the next forty-eight hours, write down the things you find yourself focusing on throughout the day. Do the nice things stick in your mind? Do you find yourself thinking about criticisms? Do you want to numb pain that comes up? If something takes up space in your mind while you are trying to focus on something else, that counts as well.

Once you have finished recording what you notice the most, look over your list a few times. Do any of the things that you focus on help you? Have you written about any acts of kindness? Then, for the next twenty-four hours, try to consciously focus on noticing nice things that people do. Can you control what you focus on? If you find negativity slipping in, try to refocus your mind.

Keep It Going! Each day, try to focus your time and attention on things that increase your feelings of happiness and goodwill. That can help give you greater peace of mind and inspire you to bring more of that to the world.

Take a Break: Free Pass Tickets

Following through on your responsibilities is an honorable, terrific thing. However, do you ever get caught up doing stuff that you don't want to do?

Saying no can be a gift of kindness. Consider how you would feel if you found out that a friend only spent time with you out of a sense of obligation. That would feel a lot worse than if they hadn't spent time with you at all. Only give your time and efforts away when you genuinely want to do so.

If you find yourself going through the motions and doing things that you want to stop, take a step back and assess whether it's best to stop engaging in things that don't make you feel good. As a symbolic gesture, write out free pass tickets to yourself and issue them anytime you need a reminder that you should act in your own best interests, even if you feel a little initial guilt. You deserve to enjoy life to the fullest and take care of your own needs. Only then can you truly help others by giving them your best.

Keep It Going! Beyond essential life responsibilities, give yourself full permission to take a break from stuff you don't want to do. Doing so can enhance your ability to be kind.

Create a Kindness Playlist

Does music give you pleasure throughout each day? Sometimes music can be in the background as the soundtrack to your life, yet it also profoundly impacts your moods, motivations, and feelings. It can even influence the actions that you take!

Spend a day trying to consciously take note of all the music that is a part of your everyday life. Do you play music as you get ready for the day? Perhaps you turn on the radio during your commute to work or choose to listen to songs on a playlist that you've curated. Do you also hear music in elevators, in building lobbies, and at work? What type of music do you hear in the background when you shop for groceries or at other brick-and-mortar stores?

You may be surprised at how big a part music can play in your day. It might not even be noticed if you're not looking for it as you sit in a coffee shop or restaurant. Yet, music does influence so much.

For a week, try to pay attention to how certain songs make you feel. When you hear a piece of music that inspires you to be kind or strive to be a better person, write down the song's name and the artist who is singing it. Add it to your kindness playlist. Continue doing this until you have a playlist of twenty or more songs. Then savor the sounds of kindness!

Keep It Going! Whether you are inspired by music or other kinds of art, surround yourself with aspirational artwork that makes you want to improve yourself and give to others.

Throw Yourself a Pity Party

We've all been hurt. We've all also experienced varying degrees of emotional and physical pain. Some types of traumas and pain are infinitely greater than smaller experiences that cause emotional distress. That doesn't mean that you shouldn't also allow yourself to feel how you naturally do after something small but painful happens. If you are sad about something, acknowledge that sadness. In fact, a pity party may be in order.

Throwing yourself a proper pity party can make you stronger and prepare you to support others when they are suffering. Think of it as a much-needed time to have compassion for yourself.

Now on to the pity-partying. What do you need to feel better? Start your own "feel better kit": Gather things like a favorite magazine, a funny movie, scented essential oils, a soft pillow, a fan, or any other item that will personally bring you comfort. Then set it aside for when you next need a pity party.

Don't feel you have to go to extremes. If your idea of a pity party is just thirty minutes of alone time where you can cry in peace, that's fine. If it involves treating yourself to a favorite meal for lunch or dinner, that's fine. Go with what you feel you need, and trust yourself!

Go easy on yourself when the going gets tough! Having a pity party helps you increase your self-compassion.

Keep It Going! Showing up for yourself is an actual act of kindness. It can also inspire you to spread the word to your friends that they're allowed a pity party too!

Make Your Own Personal Mission Statement

What would you say if someone asked you to describe your purpose in life? If they ask who you are and what you are striving to do in life, how would you answer them? What if someone asked about what you aim to accomplish this year? How does this relate to kindness and all the good deeds you hope to do? Take the time to ponder the possible answers to these questions before you continue with this exercise.

Businesses and organizations often have mission statements. A mission statement simply helps them formally define what their values and goals are. A personal mission statement can do the same for you as an individual.

Create your personal mission statement by first defining your priorities in life. What matters the most to you on a day-to-day basis? How about on a long-term basis? How might kindness manifest in your life through the choices you make each day? Get clear on your priorities and why they are so important to you. Write about them here.

In what ways do you most want to serve others? Write about some of the ways that you most want to help other people.

What motivates you to do the right things in life? Write the answers that first come to mind here.

What would you be happy doing even if you weren't paid for it?

After considering all your answers, write your personal mission statement in the following space.

Keep It Going! You may find that your mission statement naturally evolves as you change. Come back and revise your mission statement as often as needed!

Acknowledge Your Sacrifices

Prioritizing yourself is a beautiful and necessary thing in life! Does this mean that you are selfish? Of course not! Does kindness compromise your ability to achieve? If so, should you always choose a service? The answers to these questions may be extremely complex.

The truth is that you can be a very kind person but also acknowledge that life is not always black and white. There are many shades of gray in life, and the important thing is to make the kindest choices you can at the moment for all people involved. And yes, again, you need to put yourself first often in life. For example, if people don't first put on their oxygen masks after an in-flight emergency, they may pass out and then won't have the ability to help others. That metaphor rings true for most situations in life.

Sometimes personal sacrifices are necessary. They simply need to be well considered and done with a deep understanding of the risks. Do you regret any gifts you've made for someone in the past? In the space that follows, write about a situation in your own life where you chose to make a great sacrifice for someone else and then later regretted it. Describe it and what you learned from the experience.

Now think of a time when you made a sacrifice for someone else and that sacrifice was very worthwhile. What is the happy ending of that story? What did you learn from the experience? Share in the space that follows.

Now think about what both situations have taught you. What do you think will help you make an informed decision about personal sacrifices the next time one is demanded of you? How can you best protect yourself either way?

Keep It Going! Although not everyone will know the blood, sweat, and tears behind a single act of kindness, honor the strong efforts you put into the compassionate choices you make.

Redefine Who You Are

Who would you be if you didn't already know who you are? Sometimes the public personas, relationships with others, and defense mechanisms we developed hinder us from doing what we most want to do. Are there any parts of your life that you want to ultimately make over and change? Here's the great news: you can!

What is one thing that you most want to change about who you are at the moment? Write it in the space that follows. Take a moment to consider whether your initial gut reaction rings true for what you most genuinely enjoy. Perhaps you want to let go of a bad habit or unhealthy behavior. You can do it. That is just one part of you, and it doesn't define who you are as a person.

Now close your eyes and imagine who you would be without that unwanted aspect of your life. What is different? What is making you happy? How is your freedom affected by this difference? Does the absence of the issue bring new problems into your life? Reflect and write about it here.

How does this change make you a kinder person? How can it enable you to show more extraordinary kindness to yourself and the world?

In the space that follows, write three to five practical things you can do to start changing the unwanted part of yourself today. When you reimagine who you want to be and how you can still be, you can kick-start significant positive changes. That can ricochet and benefit others in your life.

Keep It Going! You are never at the end of your story as long as you're alive! You can rewrite and redefine yourself at any point. That's the power that comes with being human!

Measure the Time You Spend

Your time is precious. You only get one life and only one life-time. The value of time often becomes increasingly clear the older you get, but you don't have to wait another day to start prizing your own time. To effectively give yourself to others while having enough time and energy left to take care of yourself and accomplish your own goals, track your time to see how you are balancing your life and your kindnesses.

Next week, track how much time you spend on acts of kindness to yourself and others. You can use an app to track your time. Alternately, simply jot down observations on how you spend your time on the Notes app of your phone or a scrap sheet of paper.

At the end of the week, look at the kind of activities you do for yourself and others. Do you need more time with certain activities? Do you see that some ineffective activities are taking up way more time than you thought? How might you adjust your schedule to meet your needs?

If you find that you are running out of time for yourself, set limits on the time you spend with friends or on volunteer activities. This doesn't have to be a permanent change, and it doesn't have to be something you immediately do. After all, you don't want to let yourself or others down if you have already committed to a particular schedule for a month. Just remember that you deserve your kindness first and foremost, so keep it flowing in your direction.

Keep It Going! Time is not a renewable resource. Continue to look at how you spend time, so you can devote time to acts of kindness and continue doing so for years to come without burnout!

Show Self-Compassion in Action

What does compassion mean to you? How about self-compassion? Do you make it a point to show yourself the same compassion that you show your friends?

Today it's time to prioritize self-compassion. Prepare to lavish it on yourself. If at all possible, start by carving at least fifteen minutes of alone time where you engage in your favorite self-care practices. That might be reading while taking a citrus-scented bubble bath. Maybe it's playing a video game or going to the cinema. Do whatever you would naturally do to comfort yourself and feel good. Do this and then come back to continue this activity.

Hopefully you are now feeling relaxed and are in the mood to further show compassion for your kind self! Grab a sheet of paper and write a letter to yourself about what you want to do to make your life easier. Offer yourself the attention and love that you give to your friends when they need sympathy.

After you finish the letter, take the time to reflect on how it feels to receive compassion from yourself. Think about how powerful that can be when you show compassion to others too. You may choose to display the letter or put it in a drawer to reread it when you need to be reminded of the importance of caring for yourself.

Keep It Going! Many of us show sympathy to our friends when we would not show it to ourselves. Basking in self-compassion lets you keep plenty around for others. Do it well and often! You deserve it!

Complete the Kinder World Word Search

Words have power. Words can strike and wound. They can leave scars on the soul forever. They can also uplift someone and give them the power to change their entire life.

Look at the words listed on the following page and reflect on what they mean to you. They may remind you of a time when someone cheered you up when you most needed it or taught you about how good it feels to give extravagantly to someone you love. After reflecting on each word, try to find all of them in this word search. Circle each word as you find it. As you think of each word and search for it, consider how you can make it a part of your day. Then, after you find each word, come back to the space provided here and write your thoughts about the word.

Y	E	T	B	C	W	F	H	E	T	F	W	A	W	N
D	H	L	E	C	Q	U	R	E	R	B	O	N	O	O
E	H	T	T	E	M	L	N	Z	Z	F	Q	D	Y	I
F	V	C	A	A	W	D	Y	T	I	R	A	H	C	S
E	Q	R	N	P	E	S	Y	T	L	A	Y	O	L	S
N	R	I	Q	R	M	T	K	J	J	L	P	F	Y	A
D	T	K	N	D	Q	Y	C	Q	C	J	X	Z	E	P
Y	C	E	P	N	L	W	S	B	N	D	R	H	H	M
F	S	R	J	F	U	A	H	O	Y	C	N	H	H	O
S	K	J	L	O	V	N	A	W	X	G	O	O	X	C
M	I	N	U	H	T	B	P	Z	N	G	J	J	M	J
D	T	R	D	H	X	W	G	I	Q	U	R	C	B	B
K	U	A	Z	I	B	Y	V	Z	K	J	E	A	Q	C
S	J	Z	O	U	F	I	E	X	Q	P	Z	Y	C	I
F	Q	W	D	M	G	T	O	L	E	R	A	N	C	E

- Tenderness
- Charity
- Sweet
- Compassion
- Giving
- Tolerance
- Grace
- Defend
- Humanity
- Loyalty
- Sympathy

Keep It Going! Focus on a word that strongly resonates with you. Then try to make it a key part of the rest of your day!

Draw an Inner Map

Has anyone ever told you that you are beautiful inside and out? Well, you are! Everybody has the capacity to be gorgeous inside. It just comes down to nurturing the innate goodness we have! Let's take a look at what's inside on an emotional level. Much as doctors take X-rays to see what's really going on inside, this will be a verbal excavation to get a clear picture of what's going on inside so you can get a better understanding of your own capacity for kindness.

Pretend the following image is your body. What words would define what is going on inside you today? Do you feel like crying in empathy for someone? Do you feel like shouting with joy? What are the strongest emotions that are coming up? Ask yourself that throughout the day and come back here after a few hours.

Now, after careful consideration over a few hours, write down the feelings next to the parts of your body that you associate with each feeling. For example, perhaps your feelings of comfort while reading help you feel grounded, so you may want to write "grounded" at your feet. Explore where each feeling lives in your body. Be as honest and candid with yourself as possible. Try not to judge any feeling you have. This isn't a record of how you will be every day; it's a snapshot of your inner self today, and it can change tomorrow!

What part of your inner self feels most connected with kindness? What do you feel you can do to cultivate more kindness? How would your ideal inner map look?

Look over your inner map for today and reflect on the things you love about it, then also reflect on any things you hope to change. Make a commitment to changing anything you don't like on your inner map. Simply start by acknowledging that it exists and try to focus on nurturing other parts of yourself.

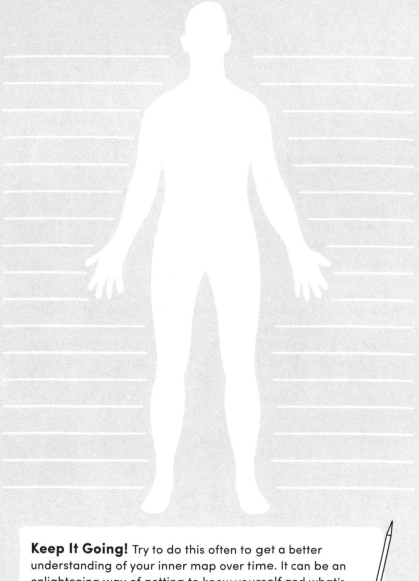

Keep It Going! Try to do this often to get a better understanding of your inner map over time. It can be an enlightening way of getting to know yourself and what's going on inside.

Lighten Your Load

Have you ever tried to carry a heavy suitcase up a flight of stairs or even up a couple of steps to an airplane? That's no small feat, and emotional luggage can take just as big of a toll on you. If you struggle with emotional baggage, you're not alone. We all have baggage. That's a part of being alive and a part of this dynamic world.

If your baggage prevents you from being your kindest self, the good news is that you can set it down, ask someone else to help you carry it, or leave it behind entirely. You don't have to let anything hold you back from being the kind, loving person you are at heart!

Knowledge is power, and identifying things is the first step to getting them under control. In the space provided here, draw an outline of four suitcases to symbolize the luggage you carry in your life. Within the outline of one of the suitcases, write about the emotional baggage you carry from childhood. In the others, write about baggage you may carry from specific incidents or time periods of your life.

Once you have identified what's holding you back, it's time to let that baggage go. In the following space, brainstorm solutions for each obstacle in your path. For example, if you are struggling to let go of how a bully hurt you in the past, it might help to write them a letter. You can choose to send it if you want, but you don't have to. Just expressing the way you feel can help you finally let it go.

Life can be so lovely when you break through barriers that hold you back from kindness.

Keep It Going! Consider seeing a therapist to help you work through any ongoing struggles with emotional baggage. You deserve a kind-filled life without the pain of the past!

Cancel Judgmental Thoughts

Do negative opinions you have stop you from being able to live life the way you most want to be living it? It's only human to have judgmental thoughts at some level, so try to be gentle with yourself if you find that you do have some.

Judgmental thoughts are not bad in and of themselves. It's a necessary part of human evolution. When we are given information, we have to discern whether it is accurate and true. We have to make quick judgments to try to keep ourselves safe. We even judge some things as right or wrong, and following that code of honor keeps us and others safe.

The bad kind of judgmental thoughts are the ones that drive a wedge between us and others or the kind that drives a wedge between us and our best selves. Society sometimes seems to sharpen the bad negative thoughts to sell products to us or get us to act in certain ways that might not be in our best interests.

Take control of your judgmental thoughts. Consider all the judgmental thoughts that have gone through your mind lately. In the following chart, under the "Renewed" column, write the "good" judgmental thoughts you have. That can include thoughts of how you wore a mask to keep others safe during the pandemic. That was a good judgment call you had to protect yourself and others.

Under the "Canceled" column, write the judgmental thoughts that you need to release and let go. That will include things such as criticizing the way you look in a dress, criticizing others for shallow reasons, or judging others for petty reasons. After you have recorded your judgmental thoughts, think of how you can let go of them. When you feel you have kicked them to the curb, come back here and cross each one out.

RENEWED

CANCELED

_____
_____
_____
_____
_____
_____
_____
_____
_____
_____
_____
_____
_____
_____
_____
_____
_____
_____
_____

Keep It Going! Try to continue to have a greater awareness of the judgmental thoughts that cross your mind. Then examine whether they are useful or ones that you need to let go.

Create Your Own Comedy

Humor all too often turns to the mean side. However, the positive power of comedy is infinite. Connecting through laughter can create bonds that tie people together forever. Making someone laugh can be a spiritual experience.

Envision how good and cathartic it can feel to have a heartfelt belly laugh. Think of the last time you got the giggles with a friend over something silly. Remember the last time you laughed until tears streamed down your face. Were all these instances of laughter caused by kind comedy? Can something be truly funny if it's mean-spirited, or is it just uncomfortable?

Can you remember the last comedian you watched who stayed kind? It's a tricky thing to do. However, it is doable, and it needs to be the responsibility of every comedian who also wants to be a kind person.

Go watch two or three comedic acts online or through a streaming service. Or watch your favorite comedy film. As you look at these things, write down any jokes that lack cruelty in the space that follows.

How are some comedians able to stay kind and still be funny? Think about that because now it's your turn. Using the kind comedy as inspiration, try to write three jokes in the following space that are both funny and kind. The more you try this, the more you will learn about what goes into creating kind jokes and resisting cruel humor. The take-away? Blissful laughter without the guilt.

Keep It Going! Continue trying to hone your kind comedic skills. Even if you have no interest in doing stand-up comedy for even a moment, it can help break the ice in social situations and be a real gift to others.

Guided Meditation: Release Anger

Anger is a significant block to kindness. It lives within you and can be a massive obstacle for moving forward with your life after being hurt. Nevertheless, it's just a natural emotion like any other emotion.

Acknowledge and honor the fact that anger is simply a feeling within you. Also, acknowledge that it's not an emotion you want to dwell on. Try this meditation to help you let go of anger.

- Get started by finding a calming haven where you can meditate without being disturbed. Relax and take a quick awareness. What are you feeling? If you currently feel that anger, accept that. If you feel out of touch with the offense but know it's a lingering problem, try to look at why you don't feel it as strongly now as you maybe often do.
- Now, imagine what a perfect world looks like to you. How does kindness manifest itself in that ideal world? What matters the most to you there? In that ideal world, how would you handle anger? What does anger mean there? How is that different from what it means in the real world?

- Take a deep breath, then focus on deeply breathing in and then out. Stay in the moment and allow yourself each sensation as it comes. Consider anger again. Focus on the source of your anger and imagine yourself filling up with the anger as you inhale, then letting it go as you exhale.
- Now, when you inhale, try to imagine a healing breath that comes in and touches the anger. When you exhale, imagine yourself letting go of a small part of the anger. Do this several times in a row. Each time, imagine yourself letting go of another part of the anger. You may even try shouting a word out loud representing the part of your anger you are letting go of.

With meditation, you have the power to connect your mind, body, and spirit with the ideals that are closest to your heart. So, with this meditation, as you let go of anger, you are also cultivating loving-kindness and extending it to yourself and others.

Keep It Going! Anger is a natural human emotion, and we feel it at all ages and stages of life. Nobody is immune to anger. Repeat this meditation as needed!

Create a Song about Kindness

Your creativity is remarkable, wonderful, and unique to you. Nobody can give it to you, and nobody can ever take it away. It's all yours, and you can express it whenever and however you want! It's your superpower. It lets you shine even if only you see the full scope of it! Today, let's channel that creativity into creating the lyrics to a song about kindness.

You don't have to know a musical instrument or dream of starting a garage band to write a song. The lyrics to a song are a special kind of poetry. They should express how you feel and what you would love to convey through the art of music.

To start your song about kindness, jot down your thoughts about what kindness means to you. Then, once you have gathered your ideas, put them together into an opening line to a song that expresses your thoughts and feelings on kindness.

Next, think of metaphors. Great songwriters often utilize metaphors to heighten the impact of their lyrics. Write down three metaphors about kindness that you can use in your song. Now consider words associated with kindness

that may rhyme or otherwise go together. Mix and match compassionate-themed words that you want to include in your song.

Next, take the time to read the lyrics to your five favorite songs. Jot down any ways that these songs inspire you. What would you like to capture in your piece that these songs manage to grasp about the human experience?

Now let your imagination go wild. Write your song. Start with introducing kindness through your eyes in the first few lines. You may then choose to write the rest of the song based on a specific incident of service that changed your life, or simply keep the focus on the power of kindness in general. This is your song. Do it your way!

Keep It Going! Try often to express how you feel about kindness and compassion in creative ways. That can inspire you and others to reach out with heart.

Celebrate Your Gifts

You are capable of giving the world your brand of kindness in a way that nobody else can duplicate. You have extraordinary things that you can do in your professional life, and you have fantastic things to offer people in all areas of your life. Your gifts as a human being can also be the gifts that make it possible for you to extend kindness in a big way!

What are some of the gifts that you bring to the world? Write about the things that you have been complimented on since you were a child. Try to write as many as possible in the following space. Brainstorm and jot them down without second-guessing or judging the impulse to count each thing as a gift. Some examples include talents, personal qualities, special abilities, physical attributes, and personal convictions.

Now think about how your gifts have benefited you in life. How might they help others in ways that they are (or could be) doing? How do your skills empower others?

What natural talents do you think you have that you could develop into top gifts? Do you want to do them? How can you better nurture your gifts so that they better serve you and others?

Keep It Going! Anytime you discover a new talent or possible attribute that you have, try to journal about it for at least a few minutes. Honor and acknowledge all your gifts!

Focus On the World You Want

Take a moment to let your mind conjure up all the beautiful goals you would create for yourself if you believed that anything was possible. Indulge your wildest dreams. Let your imagination soar to any place you want to be, even if it feels forbidden. Now consider that nearly anything can be possible if you break big goals down into smaller ones, then go after them wholeheartedly.

Given this exciting truth, we can all help build the world we truly want! Sometimes it's easy to lose focus of what matters the most to you, for you, and to the world beyond. Before you can help build your ideal world, though, it's important to know what it looks like.

Close your eyes and imagine yourself waking up five years in the future. If the outside world and your life could be any way at all, what sort of reality would you wake up to? In a journal or notebook, write down what you would see when you open your eyes and what you would experience as you walked around. Be as specific as possible. Who is there showing you kindness? Who will you share kindness with during this ideal future day? Remember, anything goes!

Now, identify five things you realized you really want in your life based on the world you just envisioned.

Keep It Going! Continue to evaluate what you want your future to be like. Once you identify what you want to experience in this world, it's much easier to plan current and future kindnesses.

Get In Touch with Your Needs

Many therapists hate the word *needy*. It's a word that is used to negate the fact that everyone has needs. Try to erase this word from your vocabulary and remove any judgment you might have acquired from society about the natural needs you have. You have needs, and you deserve to have them met! Embrace this part of your fabulous self!

For the next couple of days, try to ask yourself the simple question "What do I need at this moment?" Repeat the question throughout the day. Do it anytime you are feeling discontent. When a problem arises, ask yourself what you need at the moment. Do this when you're happy too. Try to check in with yourself in this way dozens of times throughout the day.

After a couple of days, when you feel more in touch with your own needs, talk to a close friend or spouse about what you have learned. Then ask if you can also check in with them about their needs. For the next day, have the person tell you what they acknowledge about their own needs.

You may be surprised at how much your needs are like your loved ones' needs. Maybe you are also amazed by what you learned about how different your needs are from your spouse or close friend. You deserve to have your needs met. When you make it a priority to meet your needs, you can help others get their needs met too, which is a generous act of kindness in and of itself.

Keep It Going! Your needs are likely to change over time, and that's just a part of life. Continue assessing and reassessing your own needs, then honor what it takes to get your needs met.

PART TWO

Nurture Kindness in Others

This part of the book expands on how you can spread kindness to others after embracing it within yourself. When you bring your authentic self and genuine kindness to your community, you make the world a more astonishing, loving place to be.

Learn Through Asking Open-Ended Questions

Have you ever noticed how a person can light up when some-one shows sincere concern for them? This magical spark of human communication can transform how someone feels. Active listening is a powerful way to show love and kindness with the way we communicate. One crucial part of active lis-tening is learning the art of asking open-ended questions to further understand someone. They're much more effective than close-ended questions at empowering a person to open up.

Let's take a quick look at closed versus open questions. A closed question would simply provoke a yes or no answer. As a simple example, "Are you mad at me?" is a close-ended ques-tion. It invites the person to just answer yes or no. On the other hand, an open-ended question might be "How are you feeling about what happened?"

Ask someone you love if you can have some one-on-one time to ask them some questions. Request at least fifteen minutes of their time. Then, when you two sit down, ask them a series of open-ended questions to enhance your empathic understanding of them.

Some examples of open-ended questions you may want to ask are:

- What is the greatest joy in your life today?
- What are the things you wish I would ask you about?
- What are your plans for the rest of the day?
- What would you do with your life if money was no object?
- What goals and dreams do you treasure the most in your life?
- If you close your eyes and imagine a best-case scenario of the future, what three things would you be doing in five years?

Keep It Going! Try to continue to ask open-ended questions whenever possible. You'll find it helps increase understanding, empathy, and ultimately kindness!

Set Boundaries for Kindness to Thrive

A boundary is a tool that empowers you to be kind to other people while simultaneously lavishing yourself with kindness and respect. The term *boundary* seems a bit ironic when you discover the type of closeness that it can foster between you and your loved ones. While the term doesn't sit well with some people because it seems to be about keeping others at a distance, a boundary actually leads to more significant, healthier, and stronger connections with others. The most beneficial relationships have clear boundaries that empower both people to thrive.

Setting a boundary is simply a way to communicate what you do and don't want in your life. It teaches people how to treat you. It also frees you up to realize all the ways that you can be kind to others. For example, you may decide that one of your boundaries is that you don't want to talk on the phone. Once you tell someone that you don't want to talk on the phone, you are both clear on all the other ways you can communicate. Now they know they can text you, email you, private message you, and maybe even talk over Zoom or Skype if that's okay with you.

Boundaries can be small or large. It's okay to set one limit or many. Let's explore some of the limitations that you may arrange for most of your relationships.

In the following chart, in the first column, write kind things you are willing to do within your relationships. In the second column, write kind things you are not willing to do.

You don't have to be all things to all people, and it would be unhealthy to try. Evaluate and adjust your boundaries until you feel happy, comfortable, and respected in each relationship.

WILLING

NOT WILLING

Keep It Going! Let people know how you want to be treated. Setting boundaries can seem daunting, but it empowers you to have more loving relationships.

Light a Candle

When you use a burning candle to light another one, it takes nothing away from the original candle. Both candles can then shine brightly, and the world is instantly more luminous. Kindness works the same way! Your service—no matter how small—can help others live kinder, happier, and more compassionate lives.

When was the last time a small act of kindness meant a lot to you? Think about the short-term and long-term impact it had on you. In that spirit, how can you pass the light of that kindness on to others?

Grab your planner or calendar. Draw a small candle on a date next week when you'll have a block of time available. This candle should symbolize a commitment to spend time spreading kindness. In the time between now and then, consider the best way you might spend at least a little time that day doing a kind act that doesn't take anything away from you.

Keep It Going! Do your best to spread small acts of kindness every day! Then, at the end of each day, think of how you were successfully kind and how you can continue to keep the kindness candles burning tomorrow!

Make a Celebratory Jar of Good Deeds

What you'll need: a jar, scissors, construction paper or blank printer paper, and markers

What is worth celebrating more than loving-kindness? When we call out people being good, we not only praise them for the right reasons; but we also are likely to inspire other people to follow in their thoughtful footsteps.

Here's a way to make kindness even more fun and rewarding on multiple levels. Start a celebratory jar of good deeds in your own home. If you live on your own, use it to celebrate the beautiful things that you do. If you have children, live with a spouse, or have roommates, try to involve everyone in your home in the celebratory jar of good deeds.

With children, you can make it a bit of a game where you reward each child every time you catch them doing something kind. You can have little gifts like stickers or game cards to give them when you add something they did to the jar.

This activity is simple to do! Choose a jar that you'd like to use. Cut out two-inch squares of paper. As each act of kindness comes up, write about it on one of the squares of paper, fold it securely, and place it in the jar. Then see how they add up over time!

Keep It Going! Continue filling the jar until the end of the month or year. Then start a ritual of going through it and looking back at how all the kindness ricocheted in your life.

Set New Golden Rules for Yourself

Do you think people should treat others how they would like to be treated themselves? That's a genuinely iconic sentiment, but the golden rule is only half right. Because people are all so very different, what brings comfort and joy to one person may be a one-way ticket to discomfort for someone else. To be kind to someone, try to look deeper at what they want.

Start by looking inside. How do you like people to treat you? In the following space, list the ways that you would like people to treat you that others may not like.

On the opposite end of that spectrum, what are some ways that you hate to be treated? Even if other people might not like it, what do you never want people to do to you or for you?

In the following space, make a list of ways to communicate how you wish to be treated by people.

Next, make a list of ways to start checking on the people close to you to have a greater awareness of how they want to be treated. **When you can meet people on their terms and treat them how they need to be treated, you'll find that your relationships are strengthened. It can empower you to grow closer and have better times with your loved ones.**

What matters is meeting people where they are at and understanding what they need. You may be amazed at how much a difference it makes when the people you love feel celebrated, seen, and heard in this way.

Keep It Going! As you get a greater awareness of the people you love, continue to check in with your loved ones. It's a great way to keep kindness fluid and ever-present in your relationships.

Argue Both Sides

How do you feel about unconditional love? Do you want your close friends, family members, and romantic partner to be on your side no matter what? Showing someone deeply unconditional love might be the kindest thing anyone ever does for someone.

Loving someone unconditionally doesn't mean that you will agree with everything they do and say, though. You can show great kindness to loved ones and strangers by nurturing your capacity to see both sides of situations. No matter how complex a problem, there are often two valid sides that are worthy of consideration.

Using the following space, write an argument that defends a choice that you regret. Then, write from the other perspective about why it was the wrong choice.

Now consider a situation that your friend is dealing with. Start by looking at the other point of view and write about why your friend is in the wrong. Next, build an argument for why they should have done what they did.

You are sure to encounter two different but valid opinions frequently in life. Having a calm, kind, and understanding discussion about both sides of an issue or situation can help you be kinder overall. It can help you keep friendships together even when you both see life differently. It can also help you take ownership of a desire to support your friend even in the face of sometimes disagreeing with them.

Keep It Going! Whenever you encounter a moral dilemma, internally argue both sides of the issue. You may learn a lot even if you ultimately make your initial instinctive choice.

Envision a Flowchart of Doing Good

Doing good deeds for people in your life is a fun way to move forward. To better envision how this works, create a flowchart of doing good to reason through many wonderful potential consequences of kindness. On the other hand, if you imagine the flowchart in the opposite direction, it can be a wake-up call to all the misery that might come into your life without kindness.

First, consider these fictional scenarios that mirror real-world situations and consequences:

- **Situation 1:** You have a chance to take a beautiful ring that someone has left on the ground. Choose between turning it in or keeping it. If you keep it, the flowchart will show that the person might be missing their most valuable possession.
- **Situation 2:** An unpopular person at work comes and sits next to you on your lunch break. How do you interact with this person? If you reject the person, you may hurt them in ways you never see.

A flowchart is simply a diagram that shows you what can happen based on the choices you make. Fill in the following flowchart with each situation's likely possible conclusions. Imagine all the possible consequences of being kind or being mean. Spend only as much time as you want. You are likely to soon discover that kindness is always worthwhile. Now, reflect on the joy and fun of being kind.

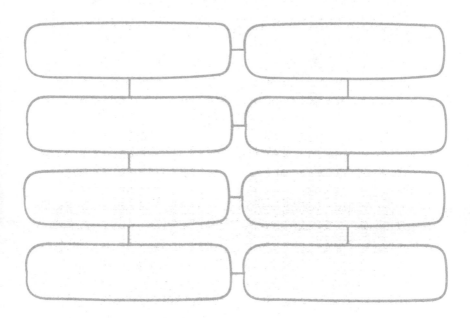

Keep It Going! Consider making your own flowchart on scrap paper to further analyze the consequences of your actions.

Write a Letter to Your Parents

The relationship that you have with your parents informs so much of what you do (and don't) choose to do in life. No matter what kind of relationship you have with each of your parents, you were influenced by their presence or absence in your life. Also, you were influenced by everything they brought into your life. Did they usually break or keep promises? Did they cheer you on or criticize? Did they mean well but do little? Did they protect you and show up when you needed them? Were they on your side? There are so many complexities to any parent-child relationship.

No matter what your relationship with your parents is like, you probably live with some things that you wish you could express to one or both of them about the ways they were or weren't kind to you when you were younger. Alternately, perhaps you regret the ways you weren't kind to them.

Whatever the case, taking the time to express those feelings to your parents can help release the inner pain that a lack of kindness created. Expressing it can also help you more fully comprehend the power that kind or unkind actions can have on a long-term basis.

Use the following space to write a letter to your parents. You never have to send this letter to them. Also, your parents don't need to be living for this to be a helpful exercise.

Keep It Going! Write letters to others who have taught you about the importance of kindness too.

Make a Record of Goodness

Do you know someone in your life who is always quick to criticize others and will never hesitate to bring you down with their opinion of all the things that can go wrong with anything you hope to do? Most people have openly pessimistic individuals in their lives. It's easy to notice when someone has negative traits. How about instead paying close attention to all the positive traits in your loved ones and all the ways they show you kindnesses?

For this exercise, choose two people whom you feel closest to. These people could be two of your children or a spouse and a best friend. Pick any two people that are close to you. Now put one person's name on the top of the left column in the following chart. Put the other person's name on the top of the right column.

Take the time to write down things you love, admire, and appreciate about each person. When writing down each trait, write about how that person uses that trait to be kind. Be as specific as possible and go beyond positive traits to offer descriptions of what makes them such a lovely person.

Examples of positive characteristics can include being gentle, energetic, and fun-loving. Now, how do they use those strengths to show kindnesses? For example, do you appreciate that the person uses their energy to do favors? Do you appreciate that they use their fun-loving personality to bring more light into your life?

Reflect on how you can be inspired by the kindnesses of the people in your life. How might you better use your talents to spread kindness? When you're through with the list, consider calling each person and expressing how much you appreciate their kindness.

Keep It Going! Make a habit of writing about any kindness that you observe and take notes on how you can follow in the footsteps of kind people in your life!

Switch Places for an Hour

One surefire way to feel more empathy for another person is to walk in their shoes. Take things beyond this well-loved metaphor and ask a loved one to switch places with you for an hour that's convenient for both of you. It might not be practical to switch places when you're at work, so you might only be able to switch places in your home life. Even that can be very illuminating, though. Just make sure it is a time when you both have to tend to responsibilities.

Ask each other for any important information you each need to know about how to successfully fill one another's shoes for an hour. Then go for it. Both of you should report back to each other and see how it went. When you do, ask each other these questions:

- What was the biggest challenge for you?
- What was the hardest part of your new responsibilities?
- How was the new situation harder than the one you're used to?
- What made this harder than it had to be or easier than you expected?
- What act of kindness would have made things easier?

Keep It Going! Although you might not want to switch places with someone else, try to imagine what life is like in someone else's shoes before you criticize their choices.

Check Your Time

Time is the most important resource that you have. You can never get more of it, and how you spend so much of it is completely within your power. The more in touch you are with how much power you have over your time, the more effective you can be at wielding it to better enjoy your life and free up more time for kindnesses.

The first step in understanding how you are spending your time is to track it. For a week, use a timer or app to track how many minutes of your day you spend engaged in the following activities. In addition to the ones listed, be sure to add in your own frequent activities.

- Self-care activities
- Sleeping
- Exercising
- Sending and reading emails
- Reading and interacting on social media
- Doing things purely for fun

Look over how you are spending your time. Does it reflect what you want to be doing? For example, which activities reflect your priorities? Are you spending the most time on those things? Consider how many minutes per week are spent on certain activities that don't promote kindness or make you happy. Consider how much time could be redirected to kinder actions.

Keep It Going! Try to stay aware. Taking the time to track how you are spending your time every few months can help keep you aware of how to best spend it.

Make a Silent Connection

Sometimes kindnesses are done in silence. You don't have to speak a single word to have a deep, meaningful interaction with someone. You communicate without words all the time every day. There are many kind things you can do without saying a single word.

Try this for a new way of looking at kindness. Spend an hour with someone in which you don't say a word but are kind to one another. Ask someone you trust to do this activity with you. It can really help illuminate what kindness can truly mean.

Consider these tips to make the most of this time. Pay attention to nonverbal cues. That can increase your empathy and help you communicate with your loved one. Think about how you are expressing how you feel without words, then see if your loved one is doing the same thing. Don't forget that you can write to each other if you absolutely need to express something silently with words.

After you spend this hour making a silent connection, talk to your loved one about what they feel. You may find that you already knew and understood how they were feeling because of the things that were communicated without words.

Respecting those cues can be a way of showing kindness to others. Nevertheless, if you don't interpret things correctly, that can lead to frustration for both of you. Clarify anything you need to with your loved one, then enjoy silent communication.

Keep It Going! Try to offer silent kindnesses often. You'll find this small gesture has a big impact.

Cultivate Empathy

Kindness is inherent in human beings from infancy, but it isn't exclusive to people. Animals of many different species express empathy and show kindness to others. Rats and chickens express sympathy. As anyone with dogs will tell you, so do your canine companions. Cats do too, and so do fishes.

Today let's embrace empathy while learning how to cultivate more of it in our lives! Start by spending at least an hour with a nonhuman animal in which you are focused on the animal's feelings and well-being.

Before spending time with the animal, do some quick research on how its species expresses happiness and sadness and learn what makes them happy. For example, if you want to spend time with a dog, learn what tail-wagging means. If it starts panting, how can you help fulfill the need that caused this action? If you are with the animal and it does something that you don't understand, try to look up this action and understand what the animal needs.

While you are spending time with the animal, try to imagine the world through its eyes. What might it be thinking and feeling about you? If it's your companion animal, you may notice things you never observed before during the focused time together. How do you think you could better support the animal? How might you express kindness to the animal? Reflect on how your empathy increased from the time you spent with your fellow sentient being.

Keep It Going! Try to accept and process your natural inclinations for empathy. When you feel them, it's best to perform an empathetic act for a person or animal.

Explore the Labyrinth of Kindness

The real world is often fraught with complex situations where being kind is not always a straightforward option. You may be conflicted about whether you can act in a way that feels kind. Take the time now to look at the most complex situations that you find yourself in at the moment.

Set aside time to get clarity on them this week. Take the time to ask the hard questions about these situations. Make sure you try to answer those questions too. Start by asking yourself these guided questions about complex situations:

If there is not exactly a kind action you can take in a complex situation, what is the nicest thing you can do?

Have you asked the other people involved what they think would help the situation? If not, ask them now. What do they think? Do you agree with them?

Have you tried to solve the situation without kindness? How did that impact the situation?

What is the kindest thing you can try to do next? What will you do if it doesn't help?

As you answer these questions, you should start to discover simple steps to take within the complicated situation. As you do, move forward and try to improve the situation. Small actions can often lead to short-term solutions, long-term solutions, or at least a temporary reprieve from the pressure you're facing.

Keep It Going! Try to do good deeds well even when you're faced with uncertain situations. You'll find that kindness often ricochets when it's shared with others.

Consider Forgiveness

Much has been said about forgiveness. It is one of the most healing forces in the world when it comes to human relationships. However, pressuring someone to forgive or stating that it is the only way to move forward after abuse or trauma is wrong and damaging. One does not have to forgive in order to move on. One does not have to forgive in order to be a fully kind person.

Look at it this way. If someone experiences a deep trauma—for example, if a loved one was murdered—many well-meaning people will say that they need to find a way to forgive the person who caused them this pain.

On the other hand, if someone breaks into a house and steals something, almost nobody would say that those people who are violated in a less severe way need to offer forgiveness to the criminal. It's a strange standard. However, the truth is that forgiveness isn't always required, and it is unkind to insist that someone forgive.

Only you can determine whether forgiveness is the right and kind thing in your life. In the space that follows, answer these crucial questions about forgiveness:

How do you feel about forgiveness?

Are there things you won't forgive?

Does the person you need to forgive offer a lot of kindness to your life beyond the bad thing they did?

Is the person genuinely sorry?

How has the person expressed their remorse for the bad thing they did? Are they willing to make amends? Can they possibly make amends?

If you can forgive and it feels right for you, offering forgiveness can be a great kindness. If you cannot offer forgiveness, it can be a great kindness to yourself to not try to force it.

Keep It Going! Forgiving loved ones for small mistakes is a wonderful thing. Just be sure to hold them accountable for not repeating the same mistakes over and over!

Expand Your Family Tree

What you'll need: poster board and multicolored markers

A traditional family tree may be something we have no control over, but kindness and love connect people every bit as closely as genetics can. Friends can be family members you personally choose to hold a special place of honor in your life. In fact, people from many parts of your life can be a part of your family tree.

Take a few minutes to think about the most precious relationships in your life. Consider who has shown you the greatest kindnesses. Think about who has shown up for you when you needed them and gave you space when you needed it.

Now reimagine your family tree to reflect the people who make you feel truly loved and respected. It should reflect those who have a special place in your heart.

Create your own family tree by drawing a tree on the poster board. Draw branches extending out and write the names of the people who belong in your family tree. They can be biological family members, friends, or anyone special in your life whom you love. Write down the names of each person you feel belongs there, then write down one kindness for each person. This should be something they did that helped you consider them to be family.

Keep It Going! When you feel a lasting closeness to someone, add them to your family tree. It can be beautiful to see it expand over time.

Create Kind Passes

What you'll need: ruler, pens, construction paper, and scissors

Have you ever wanted to reach out and do the kindest thing possible for someone you love, yet you didn't know what it would be? Try to initiate a conversation with your loved one about what they think is the kindest thing that anyone can do for them. Talk about their greatest needs and desires. No matter how well you know your loved ones, you're likely to learn some new information about what would mean the most to them.

Asking your loved ones about what their ideal of kindness is can foster a new level of closeness between you. Also, it can empower you to be kind to them in a way that they haven't been anticipating.

With information about what your loved ones want, you can start showing them the kindnesses they want. Creating these kind passes gives them a symbolic way of initiating conversations with you about when they'd like the kindnesses.

Use a ruler to draw rectangles on a blank sheet of construction paper. Write down the different acts of kindness that you want to do for your loved ones in each rectangle. Then cut the rectangles out and put them all in a greeting card for your loved one. Include a note that tells your loved one why you want to do these things for them and why you are offering them passes for when they feel a need for the kind actions.

Keep It Going! Continue to create kind passes for different people in your life to learn more about being effectively kind to those you love.

Overcome Boulders in Your Way

What would you do if you weren't restricted by your current circumstances, limitations, fears, or worries? What is the most outrageous act of kindness you would do if you had no external or internal limits placed on you? Imagine if you could make them vanish!

The first step in overcoming any obstacle is naming it for what it is. Be frank and honest about the things that are holding you back. Take the time to think carefully about this. In the space that follows, draw rough outlines of seven boulders. Then, one on each boulder, write the seven biggest obstacles that are preventing you from being as kind as you could be.

Simply identifying each problem is a big step toward a solution. Once you identify the problem, then you can go over, under, or through it to get to the other side.

Now think of the things that you can do to get to the other side of each challenge in your way. For example, if one of the issues is that you are trying to establish a healthier lifestyle to be kinder to yourself, commit to simply walking for twenty minutes per day. As another example, if you want to rescue a dog to show kindness to an animal but cannot afford it, start a savings account as a first step to having a fund for your ideal rescued companion.

Simple, painless steps will get you all the way over most boulders in your path. Take it one step at a time.

Keep It Going! Continue to identify obstacles to the path of kindness. Then proceed with confidence, because you can find a route around each boulder in your way.

Design Your Kindness Coat of Arms

A shield of armor was an accessory that knights carried to protect themselves, and a coat of arms was worn to distinguish one knight from another. It could tell you all sorts of things about what mattered most to that particular knight, and sometimes it represented what they stood for. When nobody could tell who they were with their full suit of armor on, the coat of arms stood for their true identity, or at least the identity they chose for themselves.

What are the things that stand out the most about your best self? Think of who you genuinely are as a person. Consider which acts of kindness are most important to you. What are your priorities? Which acts of kindness are fundamental to the core of your being? Which kinds of kindnesses would you want to represent you to the world? Which kindnesses help you be the best version of yourself?

In the space that follows, draw a rough outline of a coat of arms. A simple shield is fine! Divide the coat of arms into four sections. In each section, draw or write about an act of kindness that is extremely important to you. You might sketch a scene or simply write a word. This is your kindness coat of arms, so visualize what you would really like to serve as your protection in life.

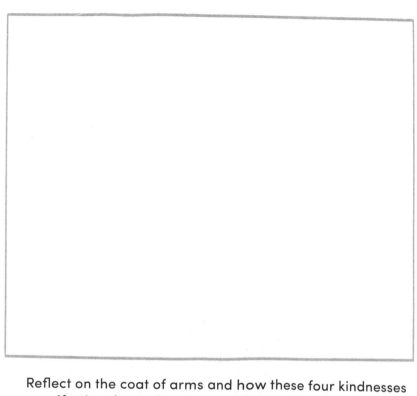

Reflect on the coat of arms and how these four kindnesses are manifesting themselves in your life. Also, consider how you wish they would manifest themselves. Do you need to make any changes in your life based on your coat of arms to make it better represent who you want to be? Take your time to enjoy and reflect on your coat of arms.

Keep It Going! For a lovely reminder of your kindness priorities, you may have an artist create a beautiful kindness coat of arms for you.

Look to the Helpers

Mr. Fred Rogers famously said that he always looked to the helpers. He remembered that, when he was a child, his mother wisely told him to look for the helpers anytime a traumatic situation happened. In other words, kind people are always there to soothe hurt individuals in even the scariest situations. These helpers inspired Mr. Rogers to live a life of kindness. Let them inspire you too!

Start by looking at the local charities in your community. You can look up the name of your town with the terms "non-profit organizations," "charitable organizations," or "charities" to see some of the wonderful things that people are doing in your community. Look at the mission of each charity to see one that aligns with your own beliefs and interests.

Contact a couple of charities that resonate with you and ask for information about volunteering. That will give you the chance to observe the helpers at the organization. Be up front with the charity about what your specific interests are too. They can usually match up volunteers with their area of expertise and interest. For example, if you are volunteering at an animal shelter, let them know if you want to walk dogs or spend time doing chores without a lot of one-on-one interaction.

Let the amazing work that people do at the charities inspire you to be proactive in helping others on your own.

Keep It Going! Continue to look for new volunteer opportunities. You may even decide to start a charity of your own someday.

Accept the Video Challenge

Seeing other people do kind things can inspire similar acts of kindness. It can also simply make you feel good! You deserve to spend time doing what makes you feel wonderful inside.

With that in mind, look up a few videos of people doing good things for others. You may choose to look up "animal rescue videos" or "random acts of kindness." Look up any kindness videos that spark your interest.

Watch three of these videos from start to finish. After you watch each video, consider how it makes you feel. Think about any acts of kindness the videos may inspire you to try. After watching a video, you may want to brainstorm about similar acts of kindness you can do in your own way.

After considering the ways that the videos inspired you, choose one act of kindness that you can do today. Take the time to do it. You don't need to overthink it. You can make today so much better for someone else and inspire them to pay it forward and brighten other people's lives today. You never know how many lives you might brighten by choosing to act now and do something kind.

Keep It Going! Make watching kindness-themed videos a habit if they inspire you to spread kindness in your community.

Look at Kindness Through New Eyes

There are nearly as many unique opinions on kindness as there are people. You can learn a lot about kindness from simply talking about it with others. Take the time to gather input about kindness from three people you respect, and consider how their own understanding of it expands your worldview. Ask them these questions:

What does kindness mean to you? Has that meaning changed over time?

_____

_____

_____

Think of a bad day you've had in the past month. What would have made it better?

_____

_____

_____

How do you determine whether someone you know is kind?

_____

_____

What's something I could do that would make you think I was unkind?

_____

_____

What makes you confident that you are a kind person?

_____

_____

What is the kindest thing you ever did for someone?

_____

_____

What are three kind actions that should become daily habits?

_____

_____

What makes one act of kindness more meaningful than another one?

_____

_____

On what occasion would you choose to be unkind?

_____

_____

Keep It Going! Try asking additional people these questions when you want more opinions on kindness.

Redirect Kindness Gone Awry

Sometimes something seems like the right thing to do, but it isn't. It's okay to make mistakes, and it's even more okay to learn from them! The important thing is to handle those mistakes with grace and fairness.

Think about the last time you had good intentions yet made a mistake anyway. Did you take responsibility for the mistake?

You are not your mistake, but it is something that you have to own. If you didn't take responsibility for your mistake when you made it, it's important to do that now. That's the best way to move on and be fair to all involved in the situation. It's an act of grace and kindness that can help make some wrong things right.

Acknowledge what you did and why you did it. That doesn't mean you have an excuse for what you did, but you might have an excuse in some situations. That's okay. You don't have to tell those who are wronged by the situation why you did it unless they ask. Nevertheless, knowing why can help you process the mistake and not repeat it.

Be gentle with yourself, and forgive yourself after you acknowledge that you made the mistake. Yes, you need to be honest and take responsibility for your mistakes. But if you're not also treating yourself well along the way, it's easy to burn out and start making new mistakes.

Reach out with an apology if you haven't appropriately apologized before. Not only should you offer to make things right, but you can also offer kindnesses to help turn the situation around. That doesn't mean, however, that you have to be friends with the person who receives your apology.

Tell the person how you envision turning around the situation. You can redirect the attempted kindness that led to the mistake to be fully kind with the next steps you take. Just understand that not everyone will be willing to accept your sincere efforts. Simply taking kind, proactive actions can help you make peace with the situation.

Keep It Going! When you make a mistake in the future, try not to dwell on it. Walk through this process of making it right, and move on to kind actions.

Embrace the Ideal Moment

Where do you want to be in five years? You deserve to be in exactly the place in life that you dream of being. Believe that, and give yourself the grace and kindness of creating a plan to make it happen. Start by really considering and embracing what you want.

Envision your ideal moment in the world. What is surrounding you at that exact moment? Are you at home or out somewhere? If you're at home, what sort of home do you have? What does it look and feel like? What scents do you smell? What sensations do you feel? Take the time to create the full picture of your perfect moment.

Think of the details that expand beyond that ideal moment. Who is with you? Where would you be if you could be living anywhere? What would you be doing? What things are currently in your life that you no longer have in this future moment? What new things have been introduced?

Now ask yourself this: What kindnesses would be involved in making it a reality? Are they ones you can do? Visualizing the perfect world can bring a greater awareness of your true wants and all the ways they can connect with others. Commit to doing one of those kindnesses in the coming week. Then come back here and do this again. Over time, create a step-by-step plan for making this ideal moment happen.

Keep It Going! Your ideal moment may change over time. Allow that to happen, and continue to be kind to yourself in the pursuit of your dreams.

Call Out the Good

Have you ever been inspired to do more for someone who expressed their sincere gratitude? It's only natural to be inspired to do more when your good deeds are acknowledged and appreciated.

Take the time to leave an upbeat and appreciative comment every time you see a post that involves someone doing something kind for someone else. When you notice someone choosing to go out of their way to be kind to you, acknowledge that with immediate praise. If you see that someone seems to be hoping for validation for something they did, provide it. In the moment, think about the kindest, sincerest praise you can honestly give and offer it.

When it comes to calling out the good, that can ricochet in many ways. It can make someone's day. It may give them the confidence they need to continue on with activism and making a positive difference in the world. It can simply make someone smile in the middle of a bad day. You are likely to receive appreciative comments in return too. It's a win-win circle of positivity, and it takes so little effort to spread this kind of kindness!

Keep It Going! Continue to call out the good you witness online and in person, and you will likely find it coming back to you.

Award Your Loved Ones

You have to lavish love and kindness on yourself before you can give it to others. This can't just happen once, either. It needs to be a habit. When you have formed a habit of loving yourself, savor how much easier it is to lavish love on others without feeling depleted.

In that spirit, take the time to give others awards for the wonderful things you see them accomplishing. In this fun exercise, take the time to design handwritten awards for your loved ones when they reach certain milestones and complete certain achievements. Then give them those awards as part of a greeting card or simply on their own.

For this exercise, start by making an award for your loved one who recently had a big accomplishment at work or school. For example, if your child overcame a challenging lesson in school or made their first home run, design them an award to commemorate the activity. You may also include a symbolic reward. For example, you might offer your child a coupon for ice cream after school to go along with giving them the award to acknowledge their achievement.

When making the award, be sure to write down all the hard work and steps that the person did to complete their achievement. Acknowledging that they earned the recognition is a very kind part of making them feel special and recognized.

Keep It Going! The next time you achieve something special, look for a physical award and give it to yourself to acknowledge your accomplishment.

Experiment with Effective Giving

You don't have to be rich to give to charity. Even $10 can do a lot of good within some charities. So don't be afraid to start small, then you can always increase your donation amount over time when you can afford to give more. You can also change which charities you choose to support.

Your mission, should you choose to accept it, is to give to a charity that does a lot of good. Determining which charity is most effective at helping others can be next to impossible. However, visiting a charity and asking questions about how they spend their donations can be helpful. There are several organizations that help people see how their donations are handled. Approach the search with a skeptical eye. Sometimes it can seem that a charity has a high overhead, but they may be doing a lot of good.

Get in the habit of researching the charities that earn your donations, and you can feel more confident about donating money. You may decide to give charity donations in people's names for six months as you experiment with which charities work for you.

Keep It Going! Try giving to charities you trust and then expand to others that also have a mission that you respect.

Role-Play for Greater Understanding

One of the most effective ways to be kind to someone is to know what it's like to be them. Ask a loved one the following questions to better understand who they are and what matters the most to them. That will empower you to show them greater kindness and understanding. You may even choose to ask these questions of multiple loved ones.

What is the hardest challenge you face every day?

What was the most fun you had this week?

What has happily surprised you lately?

What surprise was upsetting lately?

Which celebrity do you think would be kind in real life, and why?

What do you do when you want to scream but can't?

How do you prefer to express kindness to others?

How has someone hurt you this week?

What do you struggle to express to others?

When was the last time you cried, and over what?

What makes life easier for you on a daily basis?

What makes things harder?

What do you wish someone would offer to do for you today?

Keep It Going! Make a habit of jotting down questions anytime you think of something you want to know about your loved one, then ask the questions next time you see them.

Make Memories by Improving Memory

Remembering little things about the people you care about can be transformative. When you go above and beyond to remember little things like someone's favorite color or pay attention to their favorite flavors or how they take their coffee or tea, it leaves an impression. Make a list of people you care most about and list one favorite next to each one.

Name of the Person: _____

Favorites:

Food:	Beverage:	Song:	Album:
Season:	Temperature for Thermostat:	Movie:	Physical Activity:
Indulgence:	Cause:	Animal:	Thing to Do:

Favorites:

Food:	Beverage:	Song:	Album:
Season:	Temperature for Thermostat:	Movie:	Physical Activity:
Indulgence:	Cause:	Animal:	Thing to Do:

Name of the Person:

Favorites:

Food:	Beverage:	Song:	Album:
Season:	Temperature for Thermostat:	Movie:	Physical Activity:
Indulgence:	Cause:	Animal:	Thing to Do:

Keep It Going! By each person's name, be sure to write the date when you ask these questions. Come back a few months later and see how they've changed.

Draw and Reflect: Opposites

What is the complete opposite of being kind? To better understand what kindness means to you, think about what the antonym of *kindness* is to you. What does the absence of kindness look like in your mind? If you think about a memory when kindness felt completely absent from a situation, that might help you better feel and imagine this lack of kindness in a visceral way. That's not an experience you or anyone else deserves to have ever again!

Continue thinking about the opposite of kindness. Draw two boxes side by side in the space that follows. When you have conjured the image of unkindness in your mind, draw that in the box on the left. After drawing it, color the image and reflect on what would motivate someone to act in this way. Where did things go wrong and where was kindness blocked? What could have changed their mind?

In the box on the right, draw the mirror image of what you drew in the other box, except, in this situation, kindness has prevailed. What would that look like? How would everything in the image be different? Reflect on that as you draw and color this image.

Keep It Going! When you witness someone being unkind, imagine what action would counter that meanness and do it.

Be Vulnerable

Opening up to a close friend or family member about something you're ashamed of can be extremely difficult. However, it can also bring you closer to the person, and it can also show you how well prepared and willing your loved one is to show you kindness when you need it. Choose someone you're very close with and tell them you'd like to share something with them that makes you vulnerable as part of a project you're working on.

At a time that works best for you and your loved one, sit down and share something that makes you vulnerable. This doesn't have to be something huge or dramatic. It doesn't have to be embarrassing. It can be something as simple as opening up with your loved one about how much they mean to you.

If you struggle to sit down and chat with them about this face-to-face, you might want to simply text them something vulnerable. If you would rather carry this out on social media, you could also experiment with making a social media post where you open up about something that makes you vulnerable. Just be sure it's something you want to share publicly, so you may want to start small.

Keep It Going! Consider delving into the things you most want to say to several friends and family members, not just the one you chose for this exercise.

Ask a Close Friend to Open Up

This exercise, like the previous one, will help you foster closeness with a loved one through vulnerability and trust. This time, encourage your friend to open up to you. After you shared so much in the previous exercise, your partner, friend, or family member may be more receptive to what this exercise is all about.

Simply ask the person to open up to you about something they'd like you to know. Make sure they know it doesn't need to be anything dark, serious, life-changing, or dramatic. It can simply be how they feel about the relationship you have and what you mean to them. If the person doesn't feel comfortable with this, assure them that it's okay, then ask someone else.

Try to encourage other friends to open up to you too. Talk about how important you think it is to provide a safe space to each other. Remind them that you can both be more compassionate with each other when there is a great deal of trust in the relationship. Hearing what people really want to say from their heart can bring you closer together and empower you to be kinder through this newfound closeness.

Keep It Going! Encourage trust in all your close relationships by first opening up and being vulnerable, then remind your friends that you want to hear about what matters to them.

Play the Name Game

The simple act of learning and using names can go a long way in strengthening human connection. It's also one of the most basic and simple ways of showing kindness and respect for your fellow human beings. Think of the last time it felt good for someone new to use your name and show that they cared to learn and remember it. It can make someone feel special and valued!

Make a commitment to go through the following week learning the names of people that you encounter. Introduce yourself before using someone's name, though. Some people who have to wear name tags as part of their job can feel a bit awkward when people they don't know feel entitled to use their name, so be sure to respectfully ask before you start using the name of someone who hasn't yet been introduced to you.

Once you are introduced to someone, do your best to use their name once or twice directly in that conversation. That can help you remember the name with the face. If you forget, don't be afraid to ask someone for their name more than once. It's much better to ask and know, so that you can then use their name. Shortly after your first conversation with someone, try to write down the name a few times while thinking of the person's face. That'll help you remember it.

In the space that follows, reflect on your experience with trying to use names for a week. If you mess up, that's okay. Just start over again and keep trying. It will make a difference and help people around you feel important, thanks to your act of kindness.

Keep It Going! Make it a habit to learn and use people's names as often as you can!

Guess What Your Friend Would Do

Putting yourself in the positions of other people can inspire you to better understand them. This exercise can be a lot of fun. Imagine you are in the shoes of a close friend or family member and answer the following questions how you think they will answer them. Then, after you answer the questions the way you think your loved one will answer them, ask them the questions. Write their actual answers in a different color ink beneath your original answers.

Next, share with your friend how different your answers were from theirs. Ask them any questions that you may have about why they answered the questions the way they did. When you share how you guessed they would answer, they may have questions of their own.

What is a mistake that you make when you try to be kind?

What would you change about life if you could?

What do you think of the concept of veganism for animal rights?

Do you think public displays of affection are okay or inconsiderate?

What is the cruelest thing you ever saw someone do in a movie?

What is a movie that has a main character who you think is a great role model?

What novel would you live in if you could?

What is a way that you show kindness to your companion animal?

Keep It Going! Ask these questions of loved ones anytime you want. They can sometimes help you have a greater understanding of how your loved ones move through the world.

137

Play Kindness Bingo

What you'll need: five quarters

Kindness can be a lot of fun. In the spirit of a carefree approach to kindness, play this bingo game as you go through the rest of your day. Get five quarters to serve as your bingo markers. Now draw a simple bingo card by drawing a line across the top and bottom of the following space. Then draw horizontal lines and vertical lines in the space in between until you have five spaces both horizontally and vertically. Use a quarter if you need to determine the size each space should be on the card.

Now write the following kind phrases in the spaces of the card you've drawn. You can fill any leftover spaces with your own kind phrases. Then, every time you do one of the acts of kindness on the bingo card, cover that square with one of the quarters. As soon as you are able to cover up a single row, you will have won the kindness bingo for the day! Treat yourself to something really fun.

Kindness Phrases:

- Give a sincere compliment.
- Smile at a stranger.
- Donate to a homeless shelter.
- Play someone their favorite song.
- Send an encouraging email.
- Support an author by reviewing a book you loved.
- Hug someone who needs it.
- Help a neighbor with yardwork.
- Take care of an unpleasant errand for someone.
- Bake someone a sugar-free treat.
- Pick up litter.
- Serve at a food pantry.

Keep It Going! Try to play Kindness Bingo at parties by creating your own bingo cards with different acts of kindness that partygoers can do!

Rebalance Your Act

Giving to others is a beautiful thing. However, taking it too far can be harmful to you and the people you love. On the other hand, focusing on yourself too much can leave the people in your life feeling neglected or even unloved. Nobody has managed a perfect balance of being kind to others and being kind to themselves, but YOU can find a healthy balance that makes you feel happy and content without feeling pressured.

First, think of the things that your loved ones need from you each day. Start by going through your entire day in your mind. What kindnesses are simply expected from you on a daily basis? Write each one down on the "Output" side of the following chart.

Next, think of all the kindnesses you'd like to do each day that you currently don't do. What would you need to be able to do those things? How would you need to be nurtured in order to optimally nurture others? Put these things on the "Input" side of the chart.

When life feels unbalanced, kindness sometimes goes out the window. Once you've filled in both columns, you can get a better idea of how much more you need to be doing for yourself to have a more balanced life and a more realistic way of sending out kindness to the world.

INPUT

OUTPUT

_____

Keep It Going! When you are kind to yourself, it's much easier to be kind to others. Don't hesitate to ask for what you need to keep your balance!

Break Up with Unnecessary Criticism

Constructive criticism can be a positive thing in anyone's life. In fact, it is healthy, and we all need genuine people who are willing to stand up and tell us the truth even when it's unpleasant. On the other hand, unnecessary and unhelpful criticism is something everyone has to deal with at some point, and it is unintentionally cruel. It can also ruin someone's day.

Here's an example. A lot of people feel entitled to give unsolicited health advice to someone who might fall out of the norms for what someone else considers to be a healthy size. However, healthy people can come in all shapes and sizes, and you never know how active someone may be or how healthily they eat. Those who criticize someone else's size are in the wrong to do so. That will never motivate anyone to change, and it is nobody's business how someone else is living their life when they're not harming anyone else.

What sort of unnecessary criticism do *you* give to people? Think carefully. Most of us do this to some extent. Whether it's chiding a partner for a habit they cannot easily rid themselves of or scolding a friend for something beyond their control, criticism can sting and be unhelpful on top of being unkind.

Use the following space to write a letter saying goodbye to unnecessary criticism. Write down all the reasons why it is a negative thing in your life and why you want to leave it behind. Then make a commitment to stop yourself every time the temptation arises.

You can do this! When you feel an instinct to criticize someone, ask yourself if it would be helpful to them and if you are the right person to do it. If not, think again before criticizing.

Keep It Going! If you find yourself tempted to criticize someone, hold off and think it over. You can soon get in the habit of keeping unhelpful or unnecessary criticism to yourself.

Imagine Alternate History

Kindness can change the world. In fact, it might have prevented some major tragedies around the world. Start by thinking about how kindnesses might have prevented some bad things that have happened to you. Could a caring action have saved you from past suffering? There's probably no way to know for sure, but it can be helpful to imagine what might have been. Write about two or three things that may have helped prevent your suffering.

Could you have done something kind that would have stopped a bad thing from happening to you or someone else? While it's not a good idea to dwell on regrets, looking at what could have been done differently is a good way to avoid mistakes in the future. Write about it here.

_____

_____

_____

What about global history? What kind actions could have helped goodness prevail and prevented tragedies? Do you think that anything could have helped alter the course of history when it comes to the worst tragedies you can imagine?

_____

_____

_____

_____

Now think about all the things that you can do to be proactive about preventing the bad things that are currently going on in society. There are a lot of ways that people and animals are systemically abused in modern societies. Use the space that follows to list kind things and proactive steps you can take to change the world for the better. The time we are living in will be history in the future. While we cannot change anything in the past, we can build a kinder world in the present. You have more power than you may yet realize!

_____

_____

_____

_____

_____

_____

_____

_____

_____

_____

_____

_____

Keep It Going! Try to continue spreading kindness. You never know what suffering might be prevented by a simple kind word.

Apologize with Care and Sincerity

An apology is one of the best ways to offer a huge kindness to someone and absolve yourself from negative regrets at the same time. You have probably grown a lot from the mistakes you've made along the way. That's something worth celebrating for sure! However, if those mistakes have negatively impacted someone else, it's perfectly okay to have regrets, and the kind thing to do is try to make the wrong things right.

If you've ever held a grudge (and who hasn't?), you know what it is like to be unable to let go of pain that someone caused you. Whether you were hurt last week or a few years ago, think about how good it would feel if the person who had hurt you reached out, acknowledged your pain, and offered a sincere apology that expressed their true regret. Although you cannot control whether someone else apologizes, you can give that gleeful relief to someone else.

Reach out to the person you hurt with an apology that includes the following.

- Take full responsibility for your actions. Even if the other person was to blame for most of what happened, now is the time to focus only on your part in it.
- Stay focused on explaining what you did wrong.
- Offer the insights you've learned about why what you did was so wrong.

- Explain what you are willing to do to make things right.
- Talk about what you are doing to make sure you never repeat the mistake.
- Acknowledge if you know that your apology is not enough. In that case, offer a plan to move forward toward what further actions you can take to build on the apology.

Whatever you do, do not offer excuses as part of your apology. An effective apology asks, instead, for forgiveness for actions that caused those hurt feelings.

If it leads to a deeper conversation and the person wants to know what led to the regrettable actions, that's a good time to explain yourself. Let the person whom you hurt set the tone and ask for what they need after the apology.

Keep It Going! Say you're sorry anytime you genuinely feel it! It's okay to have regrets and express them. That can be the kindest way forward.

Move Past the Bystander Syndrome

Picture this. Someone falls and hurts themselves on a busy street. People keep walking because they just assume that someone else will step up and help the injured individual. That's the bystander syndrome, and it's sad and dangerous. Also called the bystander effect, it's what happens when people don't help someone because they just assume another person in the crowd will step up. Rather than acting with kindness to help others, it enables people to relegate themselves to the sidelines.

Here's the good news. You don't have to fall into the trap of being a bystander. Imagine this scenario: A coworker is being harassed in the cafeteria at work. You are just walking by on your lunch break and don't know the coworker well. How would you respond?

1. Keep your head down and continue walking.
2. Stop and call out the people who are harassing your coworker.
3. Stop and talk directly to your coworker, providing them with an easy excuse to leave the uncomfortable situation.
4. Later, privately speak to the people who were harassing your coworker about why you feel they were in the wrong to harass someone. Separately, talk to the coworker to see if they need any help or support in reporting the incident. You may also offer to report the incident yourself.

The correct answers are 2, 3, and 4. This is a serious issue, and your coworker shouldn't have to do all the heavy lifting to escape being harassed. By standing up and doing the right thing, you will help make the work environment a less toxic, safer space for your coworker and others in the future.

Acknowledge your own inner instincts as a human being to help fellow humans or animals of other species who are in trouble. Commit to taking action if you notice someone in trouble.

Keep It Going! Continue to remind yourself to take action anytime you see someone in need. Never assume that someone else will come to the rescue.

Go Beyond Your Status

Do you remember the last time a social media post made you feel good? What was so great about it? Was it a fluffy kitten video that reminded you of the absolute wonder of youth and life? Was it a post that shared in-depth knowledge on a topic that you love to read about? Was it simply a story pointing out good news in a sea of bad news? Think about those social media posts that really do make a positive impact on you when you read them.

Now, take the power to create a happy social media post for other people to read. More specifically, write a social media post with the sole purpose of being in service to others and offering a story about something kind someone did for you. If they are a social media connection, you may even tag them in it. Public praise like that can make someone's day...or even their entire month!

You may be surprised at the reactions to your post. Sometimes people on social media tend to focus on negative posts for a variety of reasons, including the fact that they may feel more motivated to comment if they feel that someone is upset or depressed. Even so, you are likely to get genuine interest and enthusiasm when you regularly create posts in service to others.

Keep It Going! Challenge yourself to write only positive, helpful posts for a week and see what kind of reactions you get from others. Kindness is contagious!

Ask to Help

As you go about your week, keep a lookout for people who look like they could use some kindness and offer to help them out. When you are actively looking for opportunities to help people out, they might seem to suddenly come out of the woodwork. If nothing comes up immediately, try to keep your eye out for a few days.

If you don't see anyone who needs help in your immediate environment, try asking your family members how you can help them that day. Better yet, if you know that a family member has to complete certain chores today, do the chore for them and leave an affectionate note explaining that you did the chore and expressing your kind feelings for them.

When you're at work, try to do a task without being asked to do it and without taking credit for it! If you have extra time on your hands at work, you may ask a coworker if they need help with anything, then quietly help them without expecting anything in return. That is sure to be remembered and appreciated.

Keep It Going! Make it a habit to ask how you can help people every day. You will make a bigger impact than you can imagine when you make this a way of life!

Develop an Affirmation to Express Feelings

We are told to deny our feelings from the time we are children. We are expected to keep calm and quiet for hours at a time in a schoolroom when our natural impulse may be to scream in boredom or cry out with a need to run. This kind of chronic denial of our feelings can only get worse as we get older, and that can be toxic to the spirit and overall well-being of anyone.

It's never too late to unlearn bad habits and embrace new ones. In the space that follows, try developing an affirmation to give yourself permission to express your feelings anytime you might feel like ignoring or denying them. This is a form of kindness to yourself and to others. Start with two simple words "I am..." Next, add in an affirmation that feels genuine to how you feel about wanting to express your feelings. If you need to give yourself permission to express how much you love someone, you may state, "I am loving. I feel love. I love you."

There are no hard and fast rules for affirmations. Your own personal affirmations should serve how you feel and how you want to empower yourself to feel. You are in control, and any emotion you have is valid. Help yourself express your emotions. They deserve to be heard!

Keep It Going! Your affirmations can support closeness and kindness between you and your loved ones. Say them often to remind yourself to express your feelings.

Measure the Energies of Each Transaction

Have you ever left a conversation with someone and felt completely drained of energy to the point where a nap sounded like a good idea? People who take a lot out of you often have problems and reasons for being so demanding of your time and energy, but you have a right to protect your precious time, energy, and sense of well-being from this sort of unhealthy interaction. It isn't kind to yourself to participate in relationships that take too much out of you.

Think about the last time someone really drained you. What was going on there? Was it your fault that you felt drained afterward? Was it because you were hiding something or weren't being your kindest self in the conversation? Was there something you could have done to make the interaction go differently? If not, consider what is wrong in the situation. It might be that the person you are talking to is not healthy for you to be around.

For the next week, check in with yourself every time you have a difficult interaction with someone. Write a sentence about every difficult transaction in the space that follows. How much energy did it take from you? How much responsibility do you think you had for why it was negative? What specific things did the person do to make you feel bad?

If you are putting too much energy into a relationship that leaves you feeling depleted, reevaluate what's going on within it. Responding negatively can take much more time and energy than the simple act of responding in a kind way. Repeatedly dealing with frustrating people may not be worth it, though. It's important to let go of people who are not acting in your best interests so you can direct your kindness and energy toward people who deserve and honor your kindness.

Keep It Going! Continue to assess how your relationships are going and how much each one is contributing to your life.

Let Kindness Take Flight

Imagine your mind as a busy airport with thoughts and emotions flying in and out. There's no way to control the emotions and thoughts that sometimes fly in at warped speed. They'll sometimes linger for a minute, and they'll stick around as long as a weeklong flight delay at other times. You cannot control that any more than you can control whether your actual flight arrives on time when you're traveling.

A kind thing you can do for yourself is simply to accept that you cannot control your emotions. You can make smart decisions and try to make choices that will make you happy, but you cannot control whether you actually feel happy. Sadness and happiness may sometimes coexist and dwell in your mind and heart at the same time. Acknowledging both the negative and the positive emotions will let the bad ones more freely pass on through.

When you start to feel really bad, gently remind yourself that all emotions are temporary, and they will pass. This is something you can also gently remind those you love. Remind your family and friends that confide in you about their sad feelings that it is okay to feel any way that they feel. Let them know that they can come to you to talk about negative emotions. Holding space for them to simply exist with their sadness and discuss it without being dismissed can be extraordinarily kind.

Keep It Going! Sincerely ask how your loved ones are doing. Holding space for the many emotions of others can be one of the kindest things you can do for them.

Let Go of Unkindness

When you hear the word *toxic*, do you imagine a trash dump with icky sludge and poisonous gases? Well, an emotionally toxic environment can make you feel like you're living in the middle of that mess. Let's take a look at things that you want to release.

If you realize that someone is behaving in a negative way toward you, evaluate the seriousness of their misbehavior. If they are abusing you in any way and on any level, cut them off immediately if you can. If you can't, seek help beyond this book. A therapist can help you find a safe way to leave a situation you no longer want to be in.

If an acquaintance isn't treating you the way you deserve, walk away without hesitation. This wonderful world has millions of people in it, and thousands upon thousands of people are out there who will treat you with love, kindness, and respect. Don't waste your time with someone who treats you in any way that excludes kindness.

If you want to try to salvage a situation where someone disrespects you, call them out on the disrespect. You can say something as simple as "Don't treat me like that. If you continue to treat me that way, I won't be able to tolerate it." If they persist in disrespecting you, cut them out of your life. A good litmus test for friends is how well they respond to your request for reasonable changes in how they treat you. If they won't even consider it, that's a red flag and a sign to release them from your life.

Keep It Going! Let go of anyone who is hurtful in your life. They are likely to be toxic to kindness and toxic to living a kind-filled life.

Take the Pilot's Seat

Take charge of things that are within your control to create a life more conducive to kindness. You are in control of more than you tend to think. You are in control of how you respond to others and the immediate environment that surrounds you in your home. You are also in control of how much kindness you dole out to yourself and others. You have a great deal of control of your day and your life. Consider how much control you have over the following things:

- **What you say:** Are you using good judgment with how you talk to others and yourself?
- **How you spend your free time:** Are you truly relaxing? Are you nurturing yourself so that you can give back to others?
- **How much you move:** Are you moving your body each day and treating yourself in a kind way? Are you encouraging those around you to get moving and celebrate the body they are in? Are you setting a positive example of daily movement for your kids?

This is just the beginning. Use the space that follows to write at least twelve things that you can control in your daily life. Beside each thing, write a short one-sentence plan for how you can start taking control of your life to build a kinder tomorrow.

Keep It Going! Examine your life each week to see how well you are progressing. Take notes on how you're shaping your life into a kind-filled life you're proud to be living.

Acknowledge a Loved One's Hurts

You can't make an illness vanish or offer any true words of wisdom when a loved one is grieving. What you can do is offer kindness. Make a list of times that small acts of kindness made you feel better even when they didn't change your situation.

If you struggle to add things to the list, try to distract yourself for a moment and then refocus on some of the most profound experiences you've had. You may think about how people helped you after a huge loss. If you have been sick in the hospital, the simple act of receiving a note or a call might have been just the reminder you needed of how much you were loved. On the other hand, it could also be something that happened on an ordinary day when something small went wrong, and it was fixed by someone else's kindness.

Now make a list of ways that you can pay it forward and similarly help people in your life feel better even when you cannot make their situations any better. Hint: Simply acknowledging that a situation stinks, that it's unfair, and that you stand in solidarity with someone can make a world of difference!

You may call or text a friend to get their feedback. How would they want you to help them if they were in peril? What would cheer them up if they were sick? They may feel differently if they are in a crisis. However, learning more about them now can help you effectively be there for them later.

Keep It Going! Let your loved ones know that you see their pain, and are holding space for them in their time of need—no matter how they might be feeling.

End the Circle of Gossip

Gossip is mean. That's just a fact. There are no shades of gray when it comes to gossip. It inevitably leads to hurt feelings and can erode close friendships. Without even meaning to, you can spread lies and unfairly help destroy someone's reputation if you engage in gossip.

Here's the tricky thing, though. Most people engage in gossip at some point because it's such an easy thing to fall into. If someone at work says a negative comment about a coworker who hasn't treated you nicely, the temptation to spread the negativity can be intense.

Even if you don't want to gossip, you may feel left out if you are in a group that gossips a lot. You may even fear that people will think you're no fun if you don't join in the accepted level of gossip that can be a part of some friend groups and work environments. The truth is that it's a lot more fun to be free of gossip, but it doesn't always feel that way.

If someone tries to gossip with you, you don't have to gossip or be unfriendly about stopping gossip in its tracks. Consider these practical solutions to tricky situations.

- Change the subject when someone tries to gossip with you. If the person persists, simply say that you don't have anything to say on that topic and ask them to drop it.
- Point out something positive about the person who is being gossiped about in a group and contradict things that you know are lies. You don't have to be combative, and you may be pleasantly surprised to discover that others in the group are relieved to see a way to get off the gossiping bandwagon.

- If you're tempted to initiate gossip about someone, vent to a private diary at home that nobody will be able to access beyond you.
- Avoid whispering in the presence of others. It can make people feel like you're gossiping about them even if you wouldn't dream of it.
- Restrict in-jokes, including all jokes that may leave others feeling excluded, to one-on-one conversations unless you are prepared to share them with others.

Keep It Going! Be gentle with yourself. If you find yourself being pulled into gossip, it's okay to stop at any point and walk away.

Extinguish Fires for Yourself and Others

One of the kindest things that you can do for yourself is to solve your problems. On that note, one of the kindest things you can do for others is help them solve their problems.

Rather than letting problems fester until they get bigger and become unmanageable, dealing with them directly is the quickest way to work through them so they can soon be in your rearview mirror.

Using the squares on the top, write about the three most pressing problems that you need to handle. Using the squares on the bottom, write about the three biggest problems that you've observed in your loved ones. Choose problems that you might be able to help them solve. You may choose one problem for three different people or three problems that one loved one has.

Once you have written these problems down, consider what it is you are doing to keep the fires of your problem burning. How are you contributing to the problem in the here and now? For example, if the problem is a rift in an important friendship in your life, you may be worsening it by simply ignoring the person.

In that scenario, one possible way to extinguish the fire that the problem represents is to arrange to talk to the friend face-to-face. Prepare to say everything that you are upset about that led to the rift. Also, be prepared to actively listen to your friend. If you were the one in the wrong, apologize profusely and witness the pain and expression of pain that your friend is facing.

For each problem, write what you think is the best next step for solving the problem. Make a commitment to take action on solving each issue within the week. For your loved ones' problems, write down how you can best be there for them on their own terms. While you cannot solve others' problems, letting them know that you care unconditionally and are there for them may help motivate them to make necessary changes in their own lives.

Keep It Going! Recommit to taking action every time a problem presents itself. When you get in the habit of proactively handling your problems, you free yourself up to be kinder to yourself and those around you.

Engage In a Positive Energy Exchange

Have you noticed that having high energy can have a contagious effect on others? This is true on a community level. When people are energized in a positive way, they tend to be kinder to each other.

Start with yourself. What can you do to enhance your energy level each day? Perhaps you feel better when you dance in the morning or hit the gym? Are you energized simply by reminding yourself of all the wonderful things in life? Whatever it takes to help you feel positive in the morning, try to do that.

Next, try smiling at people throughout your day. That's a simple way to let people know that you are glad to see them. You don't owe anyone a smile, and you should never feel obligated to smile at anyone if you don't want to do so. However, if you do feel inspired to smile at strangers, you may find that this helps them feel acknowledged and even encouraged.

Acknowledge and interact with others around you. For example, if you find someone is doing an interesting task, you may express that you find it interesting and ask questions about it. That simple attention can lift someone's spirits and at the same time allow you to be genuinely kind to someone with very little effort.

Try to be conscious of how your actions and energy seem to have an impact on others. Simply interacting with people with kind intentions can show in how you treat them, and you may find that they are responding to you with more cheerfulness than they perhaps responded to the person they were interacting with before you came along.

Keep It Going! Try to keep a positive frame of mind when you can genuinely do so, but don't be afraid of expressing less-than-joyful feelings along the way too.

Read Faces and Recognize Expressions

One quality of highly empathic people is that they look at the cues that others give. Ask a loved one to sit with you and make ten different facial expressions to reflect the emotions that they have in mind. As they make these expressions, try to identify their emotions. Write each emotion that you guess correctly in the space that follows. Write an X for each time you incorrectly guess an emotion.

Go back and write about why you thought the person was feeling a certain way for each emotion that you correctly guessed. You may ask your loved ones for clarity into why they made that expression.

Next, ask your loved ones about the most recent time they think they made each of the ten expressions. This is your chance to interrogate them about why they feel the way they do sometimes. Try to stay in the moment and ask anything that comes to mind. For example, if you are wondering which things make your loved one truly sad, you may find out some interesting facts that can help you avoid doing those things.

At the bottom of the page, write down what you feel you learned about human emotions, and how you may treat people in kinder ways in the future based on how they might be feeling.

_____

_____

_____

_____

_____

_____

_____

_____

_____

_____

_____

_____

_____

Keep It Going! Anytime someone expresses a feeling that confuses you, ask them for clarity and try to understand why they feel the way they do.

Pay It Backward

Being on the receiving end of kindness feels undeniably fantastic. There's something lovely about the genuine care that goes into someone doing a selfless act. Being aware of its beauty is the best first step to honoring that kindness. Here's an adventure in outrageous kindness.

Make no mistake about it: Kindness is a gift. In the space that follows, make a list of five people who have shown you an extravagant act of kindness. It can be recent or at any point in your past. If you're still in touch with these people, reach out to them today and let them know you are thinking of them.

If you know these kind individuals well enough to know what they may appreciate, perform that act. Trust your opinion, and be sure to include a note to explain why you want to show them your affection in this way. Instead of framing the action as a thank-you gift—especially if it is years after the original kindness—just treat it as its own unique moment.

If you're not sure what to do to pay the kindness backward, consider these simple actions:

- Give a beautifully wrapped small gift that acknowledges a passion or interest of theirs. For example, if you know they love a certain band, memorabilia of the band can be much appreciated.
- Offer to do a significant chore that can make their life easier. For example, if they have children and you know they trust you, offer to babysit anytime they need it for a month.
- Invite the person to an activity that you know they would enjoy. For example, if they love roller skating, plan an entire day around having fun at a roller rink.

Improvise and choose your own kind action. Try to do something kind for them in a new way. That can leave a lasting impression on both of you!

Keep It Going! When you feel inspired to do more nice things for people who've shown you kindness, go for it!

Make a Checklist of Universal Kindnesses

Look over this list of simple acts of kindness. Put a check mark by ones you have done in the past month. Highlight ones you want to do in the coming month.

- Invite someone who looks lonely or left out to hang out with you.
- Initiate a conversation about intersectional activism with someone who may need to hear it and discuss how you can work toward anti-oppression together.
- When you feel the need to say something unkind or snap at someone, stop and take a deep breath. Then keep the thought to yourself instead.
- Check in with a local shelter to see if you can take a dog for a walk. It can make a big difference for a dog in a shelter to get some love and attention.
- Set a boundary with someone who is asking for too much. That will be good for you and good for the person to learn about the limits that are good for you.
- Sign up for a CPR class and pay close attention so you can be prepared to save someone's life.
- Share a friend's website with honest praise on your social media networks.
- Have a loving, cheerful message put in a frame and give it to a friend.
- Call an acquaintance who may be lonely just to chat with them.

- Offer praise to a coworker in front of your boss. Be as specific as possible in pointing out some awesome things you witnessed about their work.
- Sign up for the bone marrow registry in case you are ever a good match.
- Deliver a couple of great books to a Little Free Library in your area. (Be sure to write a kind note on a spare sheet of paper and leave it in one of the books.)
- Leave a bouquet and small gift card for someone in a retirement home. If you don't know someone there, you may suggest that the staff give it to someone who needs cheering up.
- Offer to be an accountability partner to a friend who tells you they want to improve themselves.
- Make someone a homemade card that expresses some of the positive feelings you have for them.
- Choose to be an organ donor and change the preference on your driver's license.

Keep It Going! Brainstorm and write a list of other acts of kindness that you want to do in the next few weeks.

Create a Care Plan

Think of kindness as an action, a state of being, and a philosophy! It's something you can do and be. This book is only the beginning of ways you can integrate greater compassion into your life. Now it's time to create a care plan to show ongoing kindness. It's a plan for how you want to live your life in a way that honors the goodness within you and the loving-kindness you want to show others.

After trying the exercises in this book, you should know your values. Imagine how you can best live by your core values on a daily basis. If you want to spread kindness through what you say, think before you speak. In all aspects of your life, make sure you are living according to your ethics.

What are your priorities in life as seen through the lens of kindness? For example, your children may be your number one priority in life, but how can you show them kindness and instill kindness in them? Whatever your priorities are, try to look at them through the prism of kindness.

Now, thinking of how you want to see yourself in five years, what are the most important things you want to do in life? Write a step-by-step plan to fulfilling each goal that should lead you to exactly where you want to be.

Do this by setting a big goal, then breaking the big goal into more manageable long-term goals. Beyond that, break each long-term goal into short-term goals. Once you achieve each short-term goal, you should be setting yourself up for success with the bigger goals.

Kindness will take you where you want to go in life, and it will bring a great sense of meaning to each step along the way. Take a deep breath and go out into the world with kindness in your heart and mind. You deserve it, and this world can be as wonderful as you are willing to make it.

Keep It Going! Every morning, close your eyes and envision how you want to give and receive kindness for the next twenty-four hours. It's empowering to know you can choose kindness and reimagine how you need to express it each day.

About the Author

Robin Raven is an accomplished author and journalist. From the very first time she put pen to paper, she has been passionate about writing about kindness. Robin wrote her first novel when she was seven years old, and her love of storytelling has continued to grow.

In Robin's debut children's book, *Santa's First Vegan Christmas*, Dana the Reindeer discovers how we can all be kinder. Author Jonathan Balcombe praised the book as being "like a collaboration between Dr. Seuss and Grandma Moses," and actress Alicia Silverstone raved about how sweet it is.

After Robin experienced deep trauma in her life, the transformative power of kindness helped her heal. Thanks to therapy, time with her mentor, the support of other loved ones, mindfulness, journaling, and learning self-compassion, she learned to live her life to the fullest. She observed that empowering oneself and others through acts of kindness can be a path to a joyful life.

Robin has been published in *The Washington Post*, *Condé Nast Traveler*, *USA TODAY*, *Reader's Digest*, *Brides*, and many other publications. Her travel columns at Forbes.com and *USA TODAY 10 Best* are acclaimed. Robin is a member of the American Society of Journalists and Authors, the Society of American Travel Writers, and the North American Travel Journalists Association.

Robin has a BFA from the School of Visual Arts in New York City and is on track to graduate with distinction with an MFA from California State University, Northridge, in 2022. She is working on a novel and her next nonfiction book. You can read more of Robin's work at RobinRaven.com.